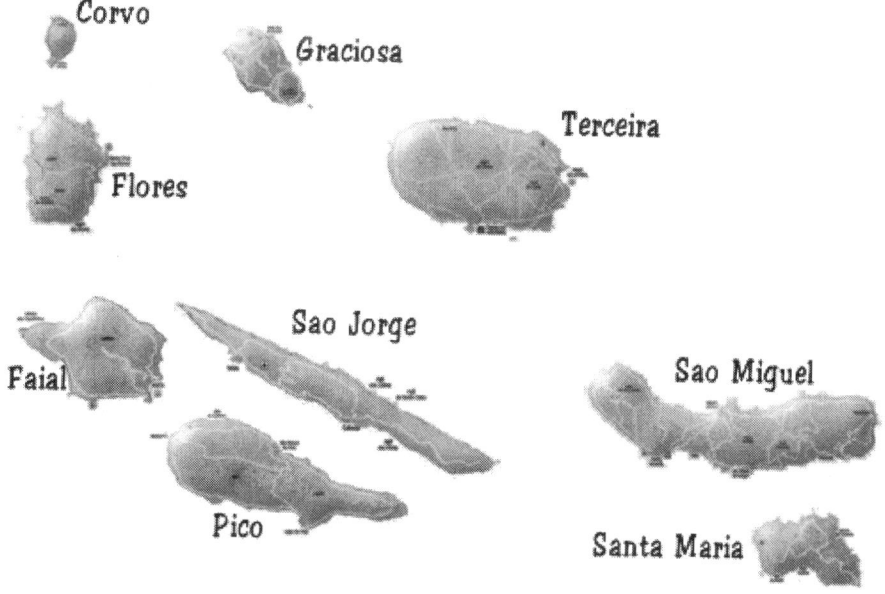

The Azores Islands

Coming to America: An Immigrant's Voyage, Mary Roy

ISBN-13: 978-1523928163
ISBN-10: 1523928166

Copyright © 2016 Mary Roy
All rights reserved. This book or any portion thereof may not be reproduced or used in any manner whatsoever without the express written permission of the publisher except for the use of brief quotations in a book review.
Printed in the United States of America
First Printing, 2016
10 9 8 7 6 5 4 3 2 1

Book Design by John Paul Cabral
Cover Design: Interior Design: JPDesigns.us
Publisher: 2016, JPDesigns.us
Editor: Sue Clark
Library of Congress Control Number: 2016902640

Three things will last forever—faith, hope, and love—and the greatest of these is love. 1 Corinthians 13:13

To Faith, Family, and Friends; and to those who taught me that these are the most important things in life.

Both children and grandchildren are life's miracles.

I am blessed beyond words for those miracles. I have received a tremendous amount of love from each and every one of them, and I love them unconditionally. I hope and pray that they know and believe that there is nothing they can ever do that will change the love I have for them. Above all, I hope they know that God is their Heavenly Father and loves them even more than I can ever love them.

    I would give my life for any one of my children and grandchildren.

    God already did that for all of them.

COMING TO AMERICA
An Immigrant's Voyage

A memoir
by
Mary Roy

Cora Coralina

Eu sou aquela mulher que fez a escalada da montanha da vida, removendo pedras e plantando flores.

"I am that woman that traced my climb to life's mountains, while removing stones and planting flowers."
                      Cora Coralina
                      Brazilian Poet

Dear Mary:

I want you to know I read your manuscript today. I absolutely love the title and your journey. Many of your experiences, I could identify with my late Sicilian mother Maria's immigrant experiences. A book has to be relatable and I am sure many immigrants from different countries will enjoy your memoir. This was a book I had to read on many fronts. I love the feeling of gratitude you express throughout your book, especially towards the end, when you compare what poverty was like in the Azores in contrast to the USA. I understand firsthand how liberating it is to tell your story. Iyanla Vanzant writes: "It's important that we share our experiences with other people. Your story will heal you and your story will heal somebody else. When you tell your story, you free yourself and give other people permission to acknowledge their own story."

There are sometimes resistance from some family members about writing your story. However, your story, Mary, was told in the tenderness way and perhaps when they read it, they will realize the importance of what you have done and that the book was/is a book of love, compassion, respect and gratitude.
Love and hugs,
Doctor Dennis Augustine,
D.P.M. /Author

DEDICATION

Dedication

I dedicate this book to my brother, Lewis Dias, 1947-1988. He was a friend, an encourager who added value to my life. He loved me unconditionally. He served many people, and brought me so much joy. Thousands of people would agree with me and would say that " Lewie made a difference in all our lives."

In memory of my parents, Clara and Manuel Dias, for their deep devotion to their beliefs in God and family. From my father I inherited courage, ambition, tremendous drive, and the joy of living. From my mom, the love of discovery through reading and learning about the world.

From my heart, I dedicate my memoir to my beautiful children, John Paul, Bernadette, Lucinda and to their children, Cecily, Jarret, Rachel, Dominic, and Jessica, with the hope that all their experiences serve as lessons that will enhance their lives as it did mine.

I also hope my memoir will remind them that the events of their birth do not dictate the conditions of their lives.

Acknowledgements

Acknowledgments

There are a great number of people I am deeply grateful for, who gave me unwavering support in putting this book together.

My editor, Sue Clark, her interpreting genius of helping me put my thoughts into words. An amazing artist. I'm deeply grateful.

To my amazing cheerleaders and best friends for over fifty years: Rita Lopez, Patti Anderson, Angela De Sousa, Mary Silveira, and sister in law, Mary Dias.

My dear friend, Doctor Dennis Augustine, who has been a beacon of deep inspiration, love, and friendship which I treasure.

My son, John Paul for the art work and designing of the book.

The multitude of friends, who throughout my entire life have told me often, you must write a book.

A special thanks to my husband, Arthur Roy, for his support and patience.

PART I

	Dedication	11
	Acknowledgements	13
	Introduction	17
	My Thoughts	19
Chapter I	Azores the Islands	23
Chapter II	Gratefulness and Respect	25
Chapter III	The Beginning	33
Chapter IV	Assistance From America	35
Chapter V	Dad Meets Mom	37
Chapter VI	Our House and Daily Routines	39
Chapter VII	Siblings Plus Twins	43
Chapter VIII	Toys and Traditions	47
Chapter IX	Jobs and Chores	57
Chapter X	The Joy of Reading	63
Chapter XI	Azorean Jobs	65
Chapter XII	Capelinhos Volcano	69
Chapter XIII	Hard Lives Lead to America	71

PART II

Chapter XIV	Coming to America	81
Chapter XV	Our First Jobs in America	89
Chapter XVI	Dreams Come True	95
Chapter XVII	Learning From My Children	99
Chapter XVIII	Active Children	101
Chapter XIX	Road to Freedom	103
Chapter XX	Taste of Freedom	107
Chapter XXI	New Steps	111
Chapter XXII	Starting Over	115
Chapter XXIII	Explorations	117
Chapter XXIV	The Family Priest	121
Chapter XXV	Spirituals Gifts	129
Chapter XXVI	The American Dream	133
Chapter XXVII	The American Hero	135
Chapter XXVIII	America The Beautiful	139

Appendix A	Friendships	147
Appendix B	A Prayer for the Nation	149
Appendix C	Letters	151
Appendix D	The Last Letter	157
Appendix E	My most precious gifts	159

Introduction

> "Of all the Nations in the World, of all the Social experiments that have been tried down through the centuries, there is no country I'd rather be a citizen of and call home than America. Where else but in the land of opportunity are people given so much freedom to pursue their dreams?"
>
> Doctor Benjamin Carson
> **America the Beautiful**
> 2013

When I think about my life, there is no other quote that speaks to my heart better than the above words. Having been born and raised in poverty, has given me tremendous appreciation for the abundance I've found in America. This is the only country I know that allows the freedom to realize dreams beyond imagination, and puts no limits on achieving those dreams.

I was raised in a small village with no running water or electricity, and into a culture that put little value on women. From a young age, we girls were groomed to become wives, to sew, cook, clean, and be a good servant to a husband.

Going to high school for a girl was a waste of time and money, and if a privileged girl did go to high school or college, she did so to get a husband.

A joke went around our village about a girl who told her parents she wanted to take philosophy and archeology. But her parents told her she needed to take sew-ology, mend-ology, and clean-ology. That was no joke, this was our reality.

As a quilter, I compare my story to a quilt. Even though I didn't always choose the pattern for each block of my life's quilt, I chose the colors that I painted the blocks with. The sashing strips that put my quilt together are the experiences I call lessons. Happy memories, sad memories, even tragedies weave that quilt and give it the strength and the shape that connects all those pieces into one unit, and holds it in place with harmony and distinction.

I thank God for my life, which is a great gift, not tied with fancy ribbons and bows, but nevertheless still a precious gift.

It is with deepest gratitude that I share my growing experiences, from a life of poverty to a life of the tremendous abundance I've found in America.

I am grateful for the freedom and the opportunity given to me and my large family, by the only country I know where we have the opportunity to realize and achieve dreams beyond our imaginations, and to raise families with joy and dignity.

Happiness is not only doing what you love, it's also loving what you do, and then continuing to set higher goals for yourself.

To say I loved cleaning houses for several years, is not true. The truth is, I loved having those jobs, which paid for my family's groceries. No matter what I did for a living, through my ups and downs, disappointments, even failures, I can never say that I never failed. I can say, when I did, I'd pick myself up, give myself a brush off, and start again.

When I take responsibility for my own decisions, even those decisions that do not turn out the way I planned, happiness comes. I have learned to own my decisions.

The opportunities given me by this great country are endless. One of those opportunities is education. Here, I found books and magazines everywhere and libraries in every city and town. I was so amazed when I learned I can own a library card and that I was able to borrow any book I wanted with that free card. What a luxury this was to me.

In my journey, I've come to realize that America does not owe me anything. Instead, America has given me everything -- the God given freedom to pursue my own happiness and my own life to the best of my ability.

My Thoughts

It's almost the 4th of July. I have just participated in the production of "Celebrate America," a patriotic show sponsored by Sunset Christian Church of Rocklin, California.

Before the one-hour spectacular fireworks show, before the Navy Seal Paratroopers jumped down to the center stage, in front of thousands of people, and before the many professional productions depicting our Nation's History, the choir, which I was a part of, sang "They're Coming to America."

Dressed in different colors, the choir showed the spectators the American Flag. I was in a red shirt that was also part of the red stripe of "Old Glory," our nation's Flag. As we sang to the residents of Rocklin and the surrounding cities on that warm July late afternoon, from all areas of the hot dog and popcorn smelling field, came children carrying flags from many nations, while we sang the opening song.

At the end of the show, I asked my son what part had touched him the most, and he said, "The opening song, They're Coming to America, and the scene with the many flags from different countries, including the Portuguese flag."

I agreed with him and as I began to explain how our family came to America from the Azores Islands in Portugal, my son stopped me and said, "You better write it down, because I've never heard the story before."

That reminded me of so many stories I'd heard from my dad, especially the last several years of his life in his '80s and '90s, and how I've regretted so many times not having recorded them.

So here it goes........

PART ONE

Growing Up

Chapter I
Azores the Islands

My journey began in São Jorge, which is one of the Azores islands, an autonomous region of Portugal composed of nine volcanic islands in the North Atlantic Ocean. Located about nine hundred miles west of continental Portugal, its main industries are agriculture, dairy farming, primarily butter products and cheese, livestock ranching, fishing, and tourism.

There are nine major islands, divided into three main groups -- *Flores* and *Corvo*, to the west, *Graciosa, Terceira, São Jorge, Pico* and *Faial* in the center, and *São Miguel, Santa Maria* to the east. They extend for more than 370 miles.

All the islands have volcanic origins, although Santa Maria has not had a recorded activity since the islands were settled in the 1400s. Mount Pico, on the island of Pico, is the highest point in Portugal, at 7,713 feet.

The Azores actually have some of the tallest mountains on the planet, measured from their base at the bottom of the ocean to their peaks, which thrust high above the surface of the Atlantic.

Up until the late '50s, only three of the islands had airports -- Santa Maria, São Miguel, and Terceira. The airport of Terceira, known as Lages, is an American Air Force base, not open to civilian aircraft until the great 1957 *Capelinhos* volcano eruption in Faial.

The discovery of the islands goes back to the 1400s. São Jorge Island is closest to Pico and Faial. The three islands are sometimes referred to as the "Triangle."

São Jorge is a long thin island with very tall cliffs, with a population of about 9,000, concentrated on its various deltas, known as "fajãs," along the north and south coasts. The island's length is 34 miles, and its width is 4 miles.

The island experienced a period of relative isolation, partially due to the poor quality of its ports and its limited economic importance. Here is where my voyage begins.

Chapter II
Gratefulness and Respect

Emilia was my make-believe name. My sister Madalena, whose make-believe name was Idalina, and I, spent hours pretending to be school teachers. We were just two very happy girls going to school, which quickly ended for us when we turned ten.

As teachers, we'd pretend our make believe houses were several stories high, with lots of windows, verandas, and gardens.

Whenever we had chores to do together, we kept our conversations focused on our pretend jobs as teachers. Other times, we played like we were the two daughters of those teachers. We loved to imagine our homes, with dining tables and fancy dishes.

In our village lived a family that had inherited lots of money from an uncle who had lived in America. The only statue on our island, located in our city, *Velas*, was a statue of this gentleman. It is in honor of his generosity to our village, where he grew up. He was also more than generous to our village church. This man was responsible for the only medical center in Velas as well.

His three nephews built amazing houses, with huge verandas, and iron-fenced gates. Two of those houses had their own chapels at the end of breathtaking courtyards, with many shrubs and flowers. Madalena and I would imagine living in one of those houses someday.

In our make believe times, we'd set our table with flowers. Maybe the table was just a spot on the ground that we had flattened. The dishes, most of the time, were a collection of eucalyptus seeds, which when they fell they'd split and form two very small bowls.

Any greenery we collected was assumed as food. When we played at Grandma's house, she would let us use a tiny iron pot she had, and that's where we cooked our make-believe dinners.

The village where my family lived called, *Santo Amaro*, was a more rural area, located furthest away from our church. Our village had only a little store, where we purchased our few essentials, such as kerosene for the lamp, soap for washing and laundry, and salt. Both our schools were there, one for boys, another for girls. Santo Amaro was mostly agriculture, with two small cheese factories. The population was about 2,000 people.

Pentecost Sunday was a very important religious holiday in our community. I remember one year in particular when our parish was preparing for the large celebration of Pentecost Sunday.

Most girls our age prepared by saving their allowances for that perfect dress and a pair of shoes to wear to the *arraial*, country festival. The festival's custom was to stroll with friends by linking our arms and to walk from one side of the *praça*, plaza, to the other. The boys and girls walked in opposite directions. This is where we'd check out each other, while the marching band played on a small stage.

The *mordomos*, sponsors, of the festivals had men serving wine, sweet bread, and cheese. That part of the celebration lasted all afternoon. Most of those who attended were invited to the *Império*, small hall, for the traditional dinner of beef, chicken, bread, wine, and an array of sweet pastries. Those pastries are a specialty in the Azores Islands, plus the traditional *arroz doce*, rice pudding.

I only attended the arraial once, when I was very young. I could see how much fun the older girls and boys were having. I loved being there, and I was determined that I would never miss it again, for as long as I lived. In order not to miss it, my sister Madalena and I made a deal with Mom. The deal was, if we could earn enough money to buy some fabric for our dresses, would she allow us to attend? Madalena and I had heard some land owners were paying a big amount of money for a five gallon bucket of genista seed. Those genista trees were excellent for fire wood, grew very fast in big clumps, and had beautiful yellow flowers, which turned into tiny pods. It would take a long time to get enough seeds to fill such a huge bucket. We also had to walk between sharp branches, thistles, and thorn bushes to gather the seeds.

At first, Mom said no. The idea of having us walk from home into the thick forest by ourselves, concerned her. Mom finally agreed because there were some places closer to the hills above us, and we promised to stay as close to the house as possible. Off we went on our new adventure. For an entire summer, up to the hills we went, with our goal in mind.

That Summer, our parents were shocked when they realized our harvest was twice as much as previous times.

To our great disappointment, with some tears, and some anguish, we found out that Dad had taken the seeds and planted them on a large mountain parcel of land we had been given as share crop property, called *ladeira*, slope.

We were never sure if Mom had told Dad about our deal, but in no way, shape or form could we ever question our father about taking our hard labored seeds.

Needless to say, we didn't earn the money to buy fabric for dresses to wear to Pentecost Sunday.

In my time, my father not only had full authority, but to question that authority was not heard of. There was only one thing we wanted to ask him. In our hearts, we accused him of wanting to look good to the landlord at the cost of his daughters' deep disappointment. However, we were only able to tell Mom that we felt that way.

We loved our dad. We saw how hard he worked, and the frustration he felt for not providing more for us children. We also knew that the fathers of our times were not our playmates. They worked from sunup to sunset to provide our survival. We knew they were doing their best. They were tough men. They ruled with an iron fist, but they were also men of honor. Men of their word. They said yes or no, only once. Woe to those children if they'd get a warning from a teacher or a complaint from a neighbor.

For example, Madalena was in the second grade. Her teacher did not live in our village. The teacher had to be driven from the city, Velas, to our village school. At times this teacher arrived late to the school, which upset our parents.

One morning, as Mom was getting the kids ready for the long walk to school, she noticed that Madalena had a big infection behind one of her ears. Mom asked her what had happened.

For a while, she was afraid to tell Mom, but after Mom insisted, the truth came out.

For some reason, Madalena had gotten to school a little late one day, a punishable offense. The teacher's way of punishing us was by pulling and twisting our ears, and hitting our knuckles with rulers.

However, when Mom approached Dad about it, he marched to Velas, and complained to the Director of Education, who in turn made sure that this teacher would never hit Mr. Dias' daughter again or she'd lose her job.

This incident made us realize that Dad, with his strict tough attitude, was also willing to defend his children, when necessary.

To compensate for our great disappointment of not going to the arraial, Mom had an idea. She packed sweet bread and cheese for each of us kids to have a picnic. Knowing how much we all loved to play with the lambs, she took us away from the village to one of the pastures our family leased, where several of our sheep and their babies were.

My brothers, Joe, Lewie, Manuel, Frank, and Joaquin, plus sisters, Madalena, Lucy, Jacinta, and I, took the long walk with Mom through the beautiful blue hydrangeas that formed walls on the side of every road to the property.

Each field on our island is divided by rows of the majestic hydrangeas, with their blue flowers.

On our way to the pasture, we sisters picked flowers, and used them to decorate the place where we spent the afternoon playing with our favorite baby sheep. The boys spent the day looking for bird's nests in the trees along the path.

We looked up at the beautiful blue sky with lots of white scattered clouds, which themselves looked like sheep. As children we imagined the clouds were the reflections of our own sheep, and their lambs.

During our time together that day, we girls forgot we had no shoes and no new dresses. We had Mom, with her bandana around her hair, her apron around her waist, her bare-feet, a big smile, and a huge heart, doing such a good job making our day as special as she could.

This became a tradition for our family. Any time we could not afford to go to the festivals, Mom made sure our day would be spent in celebration and gratefulness.

Our villagers always looked out for one another.

One afternoon, my brother Joe and I were sent to ladeira, a property we crop-shared in the hills. Dad had been given a calf by a neighboring farmer, and we were to go there to bring it home that day. The owner left the adorable little black and white animal tied to a tree with a rope, just waiting for us to walk it home. The little calf was only weeks old and was very skittish. On the way down the hill, we met a neighbor, a young married man, who tried to be funny by making a loud noise and jumping in front of the calf to scare it.

The poor animal jumped and ran off so fast, it slid the rope out of my hand and crossed a big field.

I took off running after the animal and I was able to catch it. However, when I got near Joe, he said to me, "We're in big trouble."

I told him, "How could that be, I caught the calf." Joe then explained that when that man scared the calf, Joe called the man *besta*, meaning beast, because that man had acted like a beast. We couldn't tell which was worse, the fear of losing the calf, or the fear of that guy telling our parents we had called him a name. We got home safe with our prize calf, and not a word was ever mentioned about what had happened. A sigh of relief still comes to my mind.

Dad worked away from home during the week at times. One of those evenings, he came home during our prayer time. Dad walked in as we were on our knees praying the rosary. He took off his hat and hung it behind the door. He finished the prayers with us. Meanwhile, it must have been pay-day. I noticed he'd put a wad of money on top of a tall bin. I was just out of school, probably in my early teens. Being excited, I asked Dad to let me count the money. I always liked math and thought that was a very rare opportunity to show off my accounting abilities. He agreed, much to my surprise, so I went 500 plus 500, plus, counting each note.

All of a sudden he stopped me, and told me I was doing it wrong. He allowed me to add the money again, this time, slow and accurate. He gave me and the wad of money a look of dismay, turned to my mother and said, "I'll see you later." He grabbed his hat from behind the door and left. I found out he went to return one of the larger bills that had stuck to another, and did not belong to him.

That was one of the strongest lessons a bunch of very poor kids can have, but not surprising at all, because that was my father, the most honest, honorable, hardworking man I have ever known.

Another thing we also learned from him, was to always give our employer our best. Dad had incredible work ethics. He never preached much, he lived it, and we watched him so close. It's one of the best gifts any father can give his children. Even though Dad was gone a lot, he was by no means an absentee dad. He was engaged with each and every one of us. When I see the portrayal of fathers on TV, I cringe. They are portrayed as stupid, incapable, insensitive, beer-drinking, sports obsessed, and plain clueless men.

Dad was the complete opposite of such a portrayal. He used to knock on the door when he came home. We all recognized that knock, maybe because he couldn't carry a tune. He knocked the same way, out of tempo.

As soon as he sat down, there would be one kid on each of his knees and a few on his back. Mom would try to peel us off him, but this was his only relaxation. We'd play games, usually cards, with our homemade deck. When we played school, Dad was always our student. He built us traps to catch birds in the yard, and with the same bamboo sticks, he built cages to keep the birds as pets for us. We were included in most everything Dad did, whether he was making ropes out of flax or cow hide, weaving baskets large or small, planting our vegetable garden and/or our flower garden. Dad loved flowers.

Dad was the boy's barber, and was also meticulous at trimming their nails and toe nails. In the evening, he helped Mom get everyone cleaned up for bed. Washing our hands and face, and even washing our feet. We often took turns washing Dad's feet. Because he was ticklish, his loud giggle could be heard outside the house.

One time, in America, Dad was hospitalized to repair a hernia. Before the surgery, Doctor Murphy visited Dad to go over the procedure with him, and with a few of us who were there to translate for Dad. As the doctor was leaving, he ran his pen gently down Dad's foot as a fun gesture. Poor Dad gave out such a loud laugh, he scared the doctor and everyone nearby.

When we questioned Dad on how he could fall asleep with all of us around making so much noise, he would share stories about how easy he could fall asleep anywhere. I'll share the funniest stories. Dad was in the military and one night he had guard duty in a city patrolling a certain area. The sidewalk where his post was steep. One night as he rocked forward and back, very sleepy, he rocked back a little too far, and with all his weight on his heels he skidded a long way down, landing on his behind.

Another time, he was also on guard duty. The city was at the ocean's edge, and he noticed a little boat rocking. He got in the boat and, as he described it, he had the most relaxing, peaceful sleep he could remember. When morning came, he was called by the Sergeant, who asked him. "Where were you last night, Manuel?"

He made up a false story and the same question was asked a second time.

Well, for the next week, Manuel had several hundred pounds of potatoes that he had to peel every night. From then on, he hated peeling potatoes.

Another time, he was already married, and had gotten up about 3:00 a.m., as usual, to milk the cows. He fell asleep riding the donkey to the pasture and ended up on his feet right behind the donkey. Maybe he should have been an acrobat.

Gratefulness is what I call having a mom and a dad engaged with their kids. Some say it takes a village, and for us it probably did. Not that our needs were met by the people of our village, but because our parents were engaged and taught us the utmost respect for our elders. We lived with the idea that if we were to get involved in anything our parents did not approve of, whether they were present or not, we understood there were lots of eyes and ears that could relay messages to them in an instant.

Chapter III
The Beginning

My maternal grandfather was Francisco da Rosa, born and raised in São Jorge Açores, married to Maria Margarida Azevedo. He immigrated to the United States in 1904 and worked on dairy farms in the area now known as Sunnyvale, California. Grandfather left his wife and their children to earn money in America for their support.

Seven years later, in 1910 Grandfather decided to bring his wife and their children, Maria 10, Margarida 8, and Francisco 7 years of age, to America, to be with him.

They travelled by steamship weathering storms and diseases, taking over a month to arrive on the American shore.

My grandmother, in her mid-thirties, lost all of her teeth on the voyage, probably due to scurvy she developed from the poor diet aboard the ship.

The family settled in Santa Clara County, South of San Francisco.

After the family arrived in the new country, Clara, my mom, was born on December 6, 1912. She was baptized in the mission church of Santa Clara. That church was destroyed by a fire not long afterward. A new church was later rebuilt on the University of Santa Clara Campus.

Less than a year after Mom was born, her parents received a letter from an uncle who had lived in the United States for several years, had never married, and had gone back to live in São Jorge. He was getting old, and offered my grandparents all of his assets if they would return to São Jorge, and take care of him. His name was also Francisco. Grandmother and Grandfather, and their four children, returned to São Jorge to live with Francisco, until he died.

My grandparents inherited several houses and a few other properties from Francisco. After returning to São Jorge, Grandma had six more children, for a total of ten.

Mom's siblings were, Maria, whom I'll refer to as Aunt Mary, Margarida, Francisco, António who died at age three, José, Cipriano, Domingos, Luis, and João.

About 5 years after my grandparents returned to São Jorge, Aunt

Mary was visited by her future husband Manuel Elias, who had lived in America and had returned to São Jorge to find a wife.

Aunt Mary was seventeen when they married and came to settle in Los Banos, California, where they had a small dairy farm. They also had 10 children.

Today, I have lots of cousins around the San Joaquin Valley.

Aunt Mary Elias and husband, Manuel 1920

Mom's Parents and siblings 1929 Rear L-R Clara, Grandmother Margarida, Grandfather Francisco, Mom's Sister Margarida, brother Francisco. Front L-R Jose, Domingos, Cipriano, Luis, Joao.

Grandparents took all their children to a photographer by ox cart, to send a family photo to their daughter, Mary Elias, who was living in America. Mom was seventeen years old.

Chapter IV
Assistance from America

George Elias, Aunt Mary's son, and his wife Nancy, have shared some photos with me, which include the photos of their three brothers, who served in the military, William, Leonel, and Ralph. William, was killed while serving in the Korean War.

Aunt Mary Elias, Mom's sister in America, corresponded with Mom while we lived in the Azores, and sent photos of her children. All of us kids spent lots of time both at our house and at Grandma's house looking at those photos. We loved the clothes and the fact that they wore shoes. Aunt Mary sent us used clothing from Los Banos, that she'd collected from her own children and from friends. Mom had the knack of remaking them to fit us.

When Mom and Dad got married, Dad gave her a calf from one of his cows, which she raised until she could sell it and get enough money to purchase a little sewing machine.

Sometimes, Mom would make shirts for her boys from a dress. Other times, she'd take two skirts and make a jacket, combining two colors. A photo of the twins, at eleven months of age, shows them wearing a one piece garment made from a red dress Mom received from America.

We'd take the garment apart, open all the seams and flatten the edges with the iron, and then recut it into a different garment. We had no patterns. We learned to measure from another blouse or skirt, and make it fit the best way we could. That's how we all learned to sew.

Our iron was a flat iron box, filled with hot coals from the cooking stove. The ironing board was a folded towel on the counter top.

The day we received a notice to go to Velas and pick up a package from America, was a special day for us. We couldn't wait to bring the bag or the box home. We'd open it with the entire family gathered around. The contents always had the most wonderful aroma, and filled the room with what we called, "The perfume of America."

Mom made all of our clothes, until she taught me how to sew. Once or twice a year, she'd go to Velas to purchase fabric, my most favorite trip with Mom. She made seven boys' shirts, plus one for Dad, every year, pants for all of them, plus under shirts and shorts. Lucky me, I got to stay home from working in the fields so I could sew with her. A great joy.

The one thing we loved the most was that my aunt would line the packages with newspapers. One in particular was called A Luta, a paper written in Portuguese by a priest, named Father Joseph Cacella of New York.

Not having any magazines or newspapers ourselves, we devoured every page, every article, and every story. All of that had us fascinated with America.

Our Iron filled with Hot Bricks

Me and the twins, Manuel and Lewie 1948

Chapter V
Dad meets Mom

*"Honesty is the first chapter
in the book of wisdom"*
Thomas Jefferson

My dad, Manuel Dias, and his parents had come to live in the village of Santo Amaro, in São Jorge, when Dad was quite young. They were a family of seven children, including his older sister named Maria, and the second oldest sister, Ana, who was Mom's best friend. Dad's other siblings were João, Antonio, Mariana, and Joaquim.

Dad's mom died when he was about 19. Because his two older sisters had already married, he took it upon himself to help with managing the household. This is probably the reason why he always had such a strong sense of responsibility.

Dad's family was a very hard working, honorable family. He was a handsome man with green eyes, curly blond hair, and a huge sense of humor. His family was best known by the nickname, *Palhaça*, which means clown. Dad's nick name fit him so well.

About a year after his mom died, he was drafted into the military. Right before leaving to join the military in Terceira, an island to the north of São Jorge, Dad started dating Mom. Clara was a young seventeen year old from a very good family, something that in those days was a priority in choosing a wife.

Manuel had in mind to ask Clara's father for her hand in marriage, but chances of him accepting, until Manuel was free from the military, were slim. So, he just asked permission to correspond with her.

Because he didn't know how to write very well, Dad knew he had to ask a friend to write his letters. Mom knew this, and told him she would not accept letters written by another man's hand. So, poor Dad would copy verbatim the salutation on her letters and sign his name.

The following is a cute story told to me by Mom who also had a great sense of humor.

One day she told Manuel that she had a middle name. She told him her middle name was Olimpia . She had assumed he knew she was kidding.

To her surprise, there came a letter from Terceira.

Dear Clara Olimpia da Rosa: I hope this letter...

When Dad returned from the military, someone told a story to Clara's father about Dad and his flirtations in Terceira. Clara's parents forbade them to see each other. They broke up for a short time.

One day, Clara, now 20, was sent to one of her family's orchards to pick some vegetables. Her younger brother, John, went along. They had to pass by the house where Dad lived with his family.
Clara had written him a letter and was hoping to give it to him. Instead, she had her brother deliver it. She told Manuel that if he still wanted to marry her, she was willing to wait until she was 21 and no longer needed parental consent. He agreed, and they were married one month shy of her 21st birthday.

Manuel and Clara had been given an acre of land by her parents, and with the help of his family, they built our house. The humble house was about 800 square feet, had two small bedrooms, a small living room, and a small kitchen.

Manuel also made most of the modest furniture, including their bedroom set, with a nice headboard, with four-poster legs, painted forest green.

Dad and his siblings, L-R Joaquin, Mariana, Joao, Antonio, Dad, Ana, and Maria

Chapter VI
Our House and Daily Routines

As we grew in numbers, Dad added a second bed in our parents' room, for the four of us girls.

The other bedroom also had two beds. The three older boys shared one of the beds, and the four younger boys slept in the other bed.

The mattresses were large bags, made of strong linen cloth, or sometimes made from two old quilts sewn together, filled with fine straw, or with corn husks. And sometimes, it would be just a nice layer of straw covered with an old blanket. On occasion, we'd walk over the hills above us and gather a special type of moss, *Musgão*, in the pastures there. The moss made a special soft bed. At the center of the mattress a slit was left open in order to stick our hands inside and fluff up the Musgão.

We rarely had sheets. We used old blankets for that purpose.

Our small kitchen had a big brick oven that my dad had built. Mom used this oven to bake 20 loaves of bread at a time. The kitchen had a counter made of brick and cement. Dad laid a few other bricks to make two small fire pits for cooking and to boil water. He also built a couple of shelves above the counter where we put our dishes. At the other end of that counter was where Mom kneaded the dough to bake the bread.

The kitchen floor was packed dirt. In the winter, to keep it from being too slippery, we'd gather pine needles to cover the floor. The needles had a nice, pleasant smell. Mom also boiled rosemary at times to give the house a fresh, clean odor.

Our living room had a small table against one wall. Above the table hung the pictures of the Sacred Heart of Jesus and the Blessed Mother. A long bench sat against the opposite wall along with an old trunk, where we kept all the good clothes we had for the entire family.

The living room was our sanctuary. We prayed the daily rosary there with a lot Hail Marys for the souls in purgatory and for peace in the world.

I'd love to say I found my faith in God during those times, but those prayers sometimes seemed the longest hour of a child's day -- pure torture. We were not allowed to act bored. Most of the time, we had to be on our knees. Sometimes in the afternoons, the boys and I would "play" Mass. We celebrated our own Mass with great detail. Tony often played the priest. He'd put on one of Mom's dresses and conduct all the rituals. I learned the entire Mass in Latin, which I later taught to my brother Lewie.

We had no dining room. We just sat on small stools or on the floor with our dishes in our laps. Other times we stood up to eat.

We had no electricity in our village. Instead, our lights were small kerosene lamps, about 3" tall. By those lights we did a lot of handwork in the evenings. Mom and Grandmother told us history stories and also read us stories which were always about the lives of the Saints told in books she borrowed from the parish priest. To this day, I don't know how my mom and grandmother had learned so much about history. Mom read most of the Old Testament to us and many Bible stories -- the story of Joseph being sold to Egypt by his jealous brothers, the story of Moses, Abraham, and David. Maybe Grandmother purchased a Bible when she lived in America, or maybe she was able to borrow a Bible from the parish priest. We heard the gospels at Sunday Mass, but the Church pretty much discouraged Bible reading, because the church led us to believe that they were the complete authority of what parishioners needed to believe.

We had no library, no books, no newspapers, no magazines or anything else to read, but those two amazing women not only overcame, but flourished and both Grandmother and Mom made sure their children were literate.

Outside the kitchen door was a cement tub, with a washboard our dad made out of stone. We washed our clothes there, and then hung them to dry on clothes lines.

The house didn't have a ceiling, so we could see the rafters connected to the long, thick logs across each room that held up the tile roof. On top of the roof tiles, Dad placed large stones to prevent the winds from blowing the tiles off. Each room had a small "nine pane" glass window.

Dad built the house out of stone that he and his brothers harvested from the hills. The stones, set with mortar, closed most of the gaps and blocked some of the wind, even though we could still feel a cold draft in the winter. Dad did not paint the walls in the house.

At the side of the house, Dad built a barn, where our animals slept during the winter, usually a cow, a small donkey, and the oxen.

On the other side of the barn, Dad built the outhouse between the pig pen and an area where we dumped the waste from cleaning the barn. This became the fertilizer for the yard.

We used water from the laundry tub to water the garden and to flush the toilet in the outhouse.

We made sure we'd take a trip to the outhouse just before bedtime. However, for emergencies, mostly number one, we had a chamber pot under the bed.

To prevent accidents in bed, dad would wake up all the younger kids in the middle of the night, and have them use the chamber pot in order to keep the beds dry.

Some cages sat in the yard where we raised rabbits. We had several chickens that roamed our land, but slept and laid eggs in the barn.

Dad had also built a cistern that collected water from the rain, and from the gutters. It usually was filled up from the winter rains. We had a bucket with a long rope that we drew water from the cistern.

However, due to our large family, we ended up having to bring water from one of the public fountains in the village. Sometimes, we had to go outside of the village to wash our clothes, for lack of water at home. We did have a large clay barrel in the kitchen, which we filled with water brought in from wherever we could find it. We took buckets or barrels, and carried them home from many sources.

Bathing was a luxury we could not afford. I do remember Mom filling up a half barrel once in a while and the eleven of us would take turns bathing in it. The daily routine was to wash our hands, face, and our feet at night, sharing the small wood tub with each other.

Our house was situated at the upper part of our village, facing the ocean on the front side, a mountain on one side, and fields all around.

The mountain facing the side of the house, was a great place to hike. On Sundays, Madalena and I would take our dolls and play there. On that mountain, was a huge volcano crater, but we were never allowed to go near it.

The roads around our village, and some of the streets around the houses, were not paved. In the rainy winter season, lots of puddles formed between the rocks. That was the reason why as teenagers we would carry our shoes in a bag until we got close to church. We'd go to the creek behind the church, wipe our feet and put on our shoes. After church, we'd take them off again and carry them home, safe and clean. That also saved on the wear and tear of the shoes.

As younger kids, we had no shoes, however, we still wanted to walk inside the church without mud between our toes. Walking in church with mud between my toes is something that visits my dreams, as I had to walk up to the front of the altar to be with the choir.

My Village of Santo Amaro, Lower part.

Our House in Santo Amaro

Chapter VII
Siblings Plus Twins

I was born February 3, 1940. Third child, first girl.

Brother John was almost six years old. Tony was four.

Mom said I was born in the very early morning hours while Dad had gone to milk the cows. When he got home, there I was, the girl he was wishing for. Mom favored boys. She was not cheated, for she ended up with seven of them.

I loved my birthday. I did not have to share the month with any of my siblings.

I was seven years old when Lewie and Manuel were born. They were born minutes apart, as fraternal twins. The day they were born, we kids were sent away from home. Once the twins made their appearance, some of the older kids and cousins next door, sent messages to wherever we were, telling us to come home, the babies had arrived.

Brother Joe was first to see them. He noticed one of them was quite dark. That baby had been a breech birth and was still very blue. So the announcement made by Joe to all the people he saw on the streets was, "Mom had two babies, a black and a white one." He was used to seeing black and white sheep, so that was his only reference to the babies' different colors.

Lewie was born first, small, six pounds, blond hair, fair complexion, and full of high energy.

Manuel was second to make his appearance. He was an eight pounder with dark curly hair and a dark complexion. Lewie started to walk before he and Manuel were a year old. Manuel wasn't interested in walking. He was just happy watching his brother move around as fast as he could.

One of Mom's neighbors made a comment one day, as she was walking to Grandma's house carrying Manuel in her arms and Lewie walked by her side. The lady said, referring to Lewie, "No wonder he is so skinny. She makes him walk while she carries the other one."

Mom always said they were good babies, for they entertained each other while she did her chores.

As small children, even before their school age, Manuel would follow his big brothers into the fields and try to work side-by-side with them. Other times, during school, as Dad milked the cow to feed us our breakfast, he'd send all of us younger children to fetch wood for the fire. Manuel would be gone with John and Tony, the big brothers, who were hoeing the corn fields each morning. We could see Manuel's small figure between the rows of corn where he had cleared the weeds. It sometimes made me cry, because he was too little to work so hard.

Other times, when we'd go to our property away from home, to bring wood to Mom for her wood stove, Dad would go with us. He'd send some of us home with the firewood, but he'd keep a couple of us to help either collect rocks to build retaining walls, to clear some ground of weeds, or to plant vegetables.

One of those times, Dad chose Lewie as the one to stay. Brother Joe noticed that Lewie's clothes were wet from running around between the tall grasses on the way to the property. As he was a very active kid, he never could walk a straight line and stay on the trail with the rest of us kids. However, that day, Joe talked Dad into sending Lewie home to Mom, which he did.

From then on, every time we'd go to the property, knowing that some of us would be staying with Dad, Lewie would shake the morning dew from every tree, and on purpose, he'd walk between every wet blade of grass, to make sure he'd get wet, be sent home, and to avoid hard labor at the hands of a tough laborer such as Dad.

One time, I overheard Mom and Dad discussing Lewie's trick, and they both decided the next time he did that, he'd be kept there all day, even if he was soaked. As good informers we were to each other, Lewie was told of the threat and he behaved.

We often reminded Lewie of this story and teased him by telling him that becoming a priest might have been his way to avoid the harsh manual labor we all had to endure.

In São Jorge, Azores, there are no storks. Babies come from the island of Pico, on a small boat, and some old lady sneaks the baby to the mom and dad's door in a basket. People in Pico make a lot of baskets.

When our parent's first grandson was born to my brother John and his wife, Marylou, the twins were about ten, and one day as they both sat at Marylou's bedside, Manuel had some questions.

"What if the old lady had left the baby next door?" The answer was, "The next door neighbor has no wife, so the old lady would not leave the baby there."

After a few more questions, Lewie elbowed Manuel in the ribs and told him, "Don't be so stupid. Don't you know women are just like cows?"

One thing Lewie and Manuel had in common was the love and affection for each other. As teenagers, living in America, they both left home, Manuel to the Marine Corps in San Diego, and Lewie to the Seminary in Los Gatos.

When Manuel was given the orders to go to Vietnam, he left the base without proper permission and drove to Los Gatos to say goodbye to his brother. They were inseparable.

When our parents had children, they were born at home, usually with the help of a mid-wife. Those babies were then recorded in the city of their villages. My dad would go to town a few days after the baby's birth, register the baby, and get the birth certificate. At times, when asked the date of the birth, the father's answer would be, "The baby was born the day we had a thunderstorm," or some event like that. We had no calendars or clocks.

However, giving the child a last name was a little tricky. The person in charge of the registry had been working there for a long time and knew most of the families in town. By tradition, the women kept their maiden names, which made the matter a little confusing to say the least.

Why? Because some women's families were better known than some of the men's. When Dad would register a newborn, the person in charge asked only for the child's first name. Dad's family name was Dias, but also known as Batista, from his mom's side.

Mom's family's last name was Rosa. Therefore some of my siblings' last names were Rosa, some were Batista, and others were Dias. When we all got to the United States, the American Consulate had Mom register all of them by Dias, Dad's last name. They were fortunate, because there are some families, including my first husband's, who were known by two last names. My children's dad and one brother had Cabral for the last name, and two others have used Bettencourt, same Dad, and same Mom.

Brother Joe reminded me of the story about Dad going to Velas to get the birth certificate for each new baby. The man in charge, who knew my father as a laborer, would tell him, "Manuel, I have some fava beans that need to be weeded in the back yard. Would you do that while I make the birth certificate?"

Of course Dad would oblige. Other times, it would be to plant one thing or another. When Frank was born, however, Dad had decided he would not be breaking his back for this guy any longer, so, late in the evening, he walked the four miles to this man's office. When he got there, he gave the baby's name and date of birth. The guy opened the curtains and said to my dad, "Well, the moon is very bright tonight, and I need my potatoes planted. Would you mind doing that for me while I fill out the baby's birth certificate?"

I guess it's true. You can't fight City Hall.

1947 Our First Family Photo
L-R Madalena, Joe, Mary, Tony, John, Mom holding twins Lewie and Manuel, and Dad holding Lucy

Second Family Photo
Rear L-R Madalena, Me, Joe, John, Tony
Center Row L-R Manuel, Lewie, Mom, Dad, Lucy
Front L-R Frank, Joaquin, and Jacinta
1955

Chapter VIII
Toys and Traditions

Growing up we had no toys. We children were left to our imaginations, where we lived most of the time.

All of our toys and entertainment were handmade, nevertheless lots of fun. The girls' toys were mostly rag dolls, which we made ourselves. We spent lots of time, usually on Sundays, making clothes for them, teaching them to read, and disciplining them.

The boys made lots of cows and oxen from dried corn cobs, with four nails or sticks for legs and horns. They planted grass seeds in a little square of dirt for their animals and they fed them and played with them. Sometimes they'd even plant corn for them, which ended up being eaten by the real animals, like sheep or rabbits.

One of the things we loved to do was to swing, usually in our barn on our property, sometimes in our living room. Our houses in São Jorge had open ceilings. We'd throw a rope over the rafters, drape a piece of cloth over the rope for a seat and we'd spend hours taking turns swinging back and forth, back and forth.

Going to Grandma's house down the street was a favorite outing. In her house she had store-bought furniture, and lots of tools. Grandpa would make us *galochas*, wooden shoe soles. We would make the shoe tops from fabric, and he would nail the fabric to the soles, those were the only shoes we'd have until our family moved to America. My first pair of store-bought shoes was when I was seventeen.

Not only did we pass our clothes along to our family members or villagers, we also shared shoes. I was eight years old when I got my first pair of shoes. I was the third person to wear those shoes. A village woman was the first, and a boy wore them before me.

Grandma loved to read, and she loved poems. She'd read them to me, and I would write them down.

Grandma often told me stories about when she lived in America. One in particular was about a time when she went with Grandfather to deliver milk, from the dairy where he worked to the factory.

As they were riding on the horse-pulled carriage, they saw a man on the roadside begging for food. As Grandfather began to stop the carriage, he and Grandma had an argument. Grandma told Grandfather, "The man is probably a bum and if you give him money, he'll just go buy booze."

But Grandfather gave the man some coins, anyway, and they continued on down the country road in the San Francisco Bay Area.

Much to their surprise, on the way back, the same man was sitting on the same roadside eating bread. The point of her story to me was well taken. Don't judge.

Grandma would tell me often how she loved the American culture, where everyone was accepted just as they were.

Whenever we mentioned the *moda*, trends, she'd say, "There was no moda in America. Whenever I'd go to church or to the market, I'd notice that everyone wore different clothes. Some women would wear bandanas, hats, or not cover their heads at all. Some carried purses, others didn't. No modas.

I wished sometimes I could just tell her, "We're not in America, Grandma," but I knew better not to talk back to my elders. Little did I know that someday I'd hear my own children say, "We're not in the Azores, Mom"

Grandma also taught us to make dolls out of hibiscus flowers. We'd cut one, leaving a long stem for the body, then we'd take several and layer them over as multi-colored petticoats.

The hibiscus flowers attracted lots of pretty bees, which we made airplanes out of. We'd trap the bee inside the flower, then one of us would take a piece of sewing thread, make a small loop on one end, drape it over the flower and make a small hole. When the bee tried to get out we tightened the loop, and voila! The bee would begin to fly while we held the string, and we'd play with our bee airplane for hours.

Another of those creature toys were the black widow spiders. We'd hang around the yard hunting for the biggest spider web then follow to where it was attached. Usually the big, black spider would sit there in a cobweb tube. We'd grab the web real quick, and drop the spider in a box. We'd each have a small stick, and when the spider tried to crawl up the sides of the box, we'd guide it back down.

Almost, as simple, was one of the boy's footballs, made from the bladder of a pig that had been raised and slaughtered for our consumption. The boys would fill the bladder with water, and play with the football all day.

Another thing the boys played with were go-carts. With the help of our grandparents and several neighbors, they'd save enough money to buy screws, nails, and wood scraps, and together they'd build go-carts. Most of the time, all the boys in the neighborhood would gather at our house to race the go-carts. The road going down the hill from the house was steep enough that all they had to do was sit on the cart and down it would go for a long ride to the bottom.

Very seldom did they allow us girls to ride. As with other games, go-cart racing was for boys only. But, watching them was great fun for us girls.

The *matança*, killing, of each family's pig was one of our small town winter festivities, and one of the rare times we'd have people over to our house. Several aunts and cousins would come and help us clean out the pig's intestines. We'd gather baskets full of green onions and parsley from our yard, and with them and the blood of the pig, some rice, and spices, we'd fill the large intestines with the mixture. We called those sausages, *morcellas*. Some of the pig's meat was cut and marinated for two or three days, then used to fill the small intestines. Those sausages were called *linguiça*.

We melted the fat of the pig, which became our lard, stored in ceramic containers to be used for frying and cooking instead of oil, which we could never afford.

The preparation for those winter festivities sometimes took two to three days, and having people over was special. While the morcellas were being boiled in hot water, Mom, and a few of the ladies, would play cards. We never owned a deck of cards, but we made our own with plain paper and a couple of crayons. That provided us with so much fun.

The busier time of the year was always harvest time. Corn was our biggest staple, corn bread our number one food.

As the family grew, Mom would bake bread, two to three times a week, always a good day for us kids. She'd make little individual loaves for us. Other times, we'd bake some corn ears in the brick oven and we'd always save an ear for those who were absent.

We'd also bake sweet potatoes for our dinner, a favorite of mine. Once in a while, we had milk. Other times we had some fish, which we grilled over the bricks.

In the summertime, we'd go down to the beach and buy many

baskets full of mackerel. We'd dry and store the mackerel to eat during the winter months.

Fish is a favorite food for the people of the Azores. Living so close to the ocean was a blessing.

Chicharros, mackerel, deep fried, barbecued or grilled is still a delicacy for all of us. Then there are the *lapas*, lipids, a delicacy indeed.

I have a story about going down to the ocean's rocky waters to get some lipids, similar to abalones. They attach themselves to the rocks below the ocean surface, and one has to use a type of chisel to pry them off. We also had to make sure the tide was as low as it gets, so we could find them.

I was 15 years old when Mom and I decided to go fishing for lapas. The tide was perfect when we got there. We caught quite a few. Mom wrapped them up in her apron, then tied the apron strings around making a nice package. We got ready to leave. However, the tide was now very high, and we were trapped between the ocean and the high cliff. We had no other choice than the cliff, a very steep, rocky hill with little shrubs to hold on to. We started climbing, a few steps at a time, to avoid the erosion from throwing us into the ocean. I went my way, she went hers. We seldom looked at each other. She'd move the package of lapas a few feet in front of her, as she climbed. We both maneuvered our way to safety. However it didn't turn out to be that easy.

Mom had nothing better to do, but to tell me the dangers of women soaking their feet in ocean water during a certain time of the month, "Your blood can pool in your legs at first, then your legs turn purple and you may die." Thanks, Mom, "We should have drowned while we had the opportunity, since I will die, anyway." She said not a word.

I refused to walk home with her. I kept a good distance so I could pray that God would not kill me for wanting to have my privacy. Every once in a while, I'd look to see if my legs were turning purple, but they only got to a beet red color from the hot sun.

Another adventure with Mom again, had to do with the ocean. I believe she got the joy of fishing from all her brothers, who were good fisherman. Too bad they forgot to teach her how.

One day, Mom and I took off to fish for moray eels, another delicacy of the islands. Mom's father had made her a special tool for this purpose, a large tweezer with sharp teeth from nails. With bait in hand, we took off for *Portinho*, little port. Soon after we got there, we could see the moray in the crevices of the large rocks on the beach. The first one Mom tried to catch, instead of grabbing its head with the tweezers, she caught the middle of its long body. The serpent started to fight, by wrapping up all around the tool. Mom yelled and let the tool and the poor scared moray go back to its environment. We came home safe, laughing all the way, but empty handed.

Mom also had the knack of making soup out of almost anything. We grew kale, turnips, and other vegetables. Our meals were simple but we were never sent to bed hungry.
Her soups were what we call, "Boiled dinners", vegetables, some potatoes, squash and lots of sauce, poured in a tureen over cubed bread. To add flavor, Mom would add a tablespoon of lard as flavor, when there was no meat.

The islands have no wild life, except for the multitude of rabbits, rats, mice, and birds, which did a lot of damage to our crops. We had to set traps to rid ourselves of some of them. However, the rabbits were great for food. Brother Tony made us some nice traps from thin wire lassos that we placed on the rabbit trails in the evening.

We had to get up before the men went to milk the cows, as they would always have their dogs with them, and we had to get to the rabbits before they became the dogs' breakfast. Mom would marinate the meat overnight and roast the rabbit in the oven. A delicious dinner.

Breakfast was often the traditional *açorda*, bread soup. Mom would sauté onion, garlic, and parsley, add water, salt and pepper, and some spices. She'd bring it to a boil, then pour the soup into a tureen, or large casserole, in which she'd already put several layers of bread. We ate the açorda with some grilled fish. Sometimes, we had eggs from our few chickens, but we also used the eggs as a trade for other small purchases.

Once in a while, instead of soup, we used milk that was boiled first. But this was a much more expensive meal.

One of the most popular traditions on the Azores Islands, is the festival of *Espírito Santo*, Holy Ghost. Concentrated in the many *Impérios*, Chapels, around the islands, each festival occurred every Sunday during the seven weeks after Easter, and culminated on the seventh Sunday, Pentecost.

This tradition goes back to the 14th century, when Queen Isabel of Portugal promised to feed the poor with meat, bread, and wine, if her son, Henry, would remain loyal to her after the death of her husband, the King. Her wish was granted and in gratitude and devotion she kept her promise.

That tradition continued, which is usually a covenant or promise, made to the Holy Spirit, to feed the poor if a son returns from the war safely, or a healing takes place. Sometimes, those promises were made in hopeless situations, so, when a miracle happened, everyone celebrated.

A silver and gold crown covered with precious stones, with a small dove on top representing the Holy Spirit, was brought from the church to the house of the family that made the promise to keep it in a place of honor. Neighbors and friends were invited to gather at this house every evening for one week to pray the rosary, after which they played games till late at night.

Preparation for the meal would often take several days. Neighbors, family and friends would get together and bake bread starting in midweek, in the family's wood burning, brick oven, which would usually accommodate several loaves at a time. One of the men in the village would shoot off a fire cracker, after each batch, so everyone in the village could participate, in a small way, in what was going on.

The children, dressed in their Sunday best clothes, gathered on Sunday morning at the house where the crown was located. Sometimes it became an all-girl celebration, other times, all-boy, and yet other times adult males, all by invitation. The procession through town began at that house. In front of the procession, a strong man would carry the Holy Spirit flag. On each side of the flag a man carried a wooden pole about six feet long. Four poles, each in the shape of a square, were held by the children. In the square three children walked, one carried the crown. On the right a child carried the scepter, and on the left a child carried a sword.

The flag, crown, sword, and pole, or staff, are symbols of royalty.

The rest of the children, followed behind the four pole square, followed by the band, composed of thirty or forty musicians. After the band, adults formed the rest of the parade.

When the procession reached the church, the crown was placed on the altar inside the church. After mass, the child who carried the crown was asked to approach the priest and kneel down. The priest placed the crown on the child's head. Then, those in the procession formed again and marched through the village, back to the house where the procession had begun. And all were fed *soupas* with sweet bead and wine. *Soupas* is roasted meat with meat sauce poured over home baked bread that was sliced.

I loved following the procession. The music played by the band was very special. My favorite music still is what Portuguese marching bands play, even in California, being the only music we'd heard until we came to America.

Brother Tony played the trombone in our village marching band and taught me how to read the music.

During the last two weeks of the festive season, the celebrations got more elaborate. The entire village got fed on those two weekends. In my village a cow or steer, was raised for the festive celebration of the Holy Ghost to be a big part of the meal.

I was privileged to be invited to participate in the preparation of two different festivals in my village.

At those festivals, we filled huge baskets lined with white linen and decorated with flowers, with sweet bread and cheese. Villagers carried the baskets in the procession to the village's *Império*, small hall, on Saturday afternoon. Some were loaded on ox carts that had been decorated with colorful bandanas borrowed from the women of the village, in lieu of flags. Even the oxen's horns were decorated with paper flowers and ribbons. Everyone in the village was invited to eat sweet bread and cheese, with wine.

On the following Sunday, the festivities continued, as long as the food lasted.

A more modern celebration of the Holy Ghost exists in the United States, especially in the Portuguese communities of California. A young girl is elected to be crowned queen of each festival of her own town. She's adorned with an elaborate gown, like a beautiful bride. The queen wears a royal-like cape, like the richest queens of long ago. This appears in my view, to be more like a fashion show, however because so many of our Azores immigrants are spread out in different parts of America, this is a great opportunity to connect with family and friends. The parade winds its way from the church to the town's Portuguese Hall. There, the people in the Portuguese club serve the traditional soupas.

Religious pilgrimages are a tradition of the Azores' Catholic communities, and are linked to catastrophes such as earthquakes and volcanic eruptions. The pilgrimage of the *Fajã da Caldeira de Santo Cristo* is very popular. Many of the faithful walk between religious sanctuaries, praying, meditating, and stopping for mass at a local church.

Dad made that pilgrimage every year, a few days trip by foot. Caldeira, a village in the northern part of our island, is the only place in the archipelago where clams exist. Our family always looked forward to Dad coming home with a huge sack of fresh clams for our dinner.

Most of our social activities were around church, singing in the choir, teaching catechism, attending novenas. We lived pretty far from our church. The trip to and from was a great opportunity for us kids to walk with friends.

The preparation for the birth of Jesus each year was a wonderful time. We prepared by having evening worship services at our church, during the month of December, the Christmas songs gave us great joy. On those trips to church, Dad usually went with us. The nights were so dark, and the roads muddy from the rains. The only light we had was the moonlight, when the moon was visible. On darker nights without the moonlight, Dad would take a lit torch from the stove and he would wave it back and forth in order for us to watch where we stepped, and protect us from breaking too many toe nails.

Villagers turned their living rooms into nativity scenes. On the main altar in every church, parishioners could enjoy the nativity scenes also created by the local people. Several men, women, and children would spend months making figures out of clay, that they would collect from the mountains around the village. The people would dry, then paint the figures they made which represented Mary, Joseph, baby Jesus, the cows, the donkey, and the sheep, well spread-out around the nativity scene that was created with grass, dirt, and shrubs. The houses and churches were made out of construction paper.

The people would put a star at the top of the tallest mountain made of dirt and grass to guide the three wise men who wouldn't get there until January 6. We celebrated their arrival by going from house to house singing and dancing on that day.

On Christmas day, we'd visit lots of houses to admire the beautiful *Presépios*, Nativity Scenes, which had taken so many days of preparation. Our family always made our own Nativity Scene on Christmas Eve.

We, as children could not go to bed until after the midnight Mass.

I remember one Christmas season when the rain didn't appear to want to stop. However, one of my brothers and I went up to dig for clay to build our Nativity Scene figurines. We had no problem bringing the clay home, which had been softened due to the rains.

We made our cows, sheep, and shepherds, then laid them out to dry in order to paint them later on. Much to our surprise, Mom was the first one to check our animals the next morning. Her laughter was infectious, when she saw all the figures had dried in strange shapes from being made in soft, wet clay. She said, "They look like turds."

We had a box of Christmas cards Aunt Mary Elias had sent us through the years, very colorful, with angels, baby Jesus and other pictures that we were trying to illustrate from clay. Mom allowed us to stand up the cards around our presépio. We celebrated the season with amazing joy.

Our Christmas traditions never included gifts or presents. We heard later as we grew older, that a tradition for each child was to leave a shoe on the hearth on Christmas Eve. On Christmas morning the shoes would be filled with candy. But since all of us did not have shoes, we didn't participate in the traditions. Besides, we knew our parents had no money for candy or any other trinkets to give us. The thought of putting that kind of pressure on our parents discouraged us to ever find out what the possibilities could have been if we'd put shoes out on Christmas Eve.

During the last couple of years before I left the Azores, I sang in the choir, a joy and a privilege. The last song I learned was, and is, my favorite, Silent Night.

A few times a year, usually during Lent, there'd be an opportunity to attend a "High Mass," either at our church or another village. Because of the beautiful organ music, an all men choir, and the many priests and deacons at the altar, the Mass was a festive occasion for us. The chosen priest would give his sermon from a tall pulpit in the middle of the church. While he made his way up the stairway to the pulpit, a soloist would sing "Avé Maria." One of the three soloists in our village, when I was a teenager, was John Cabral. I heard him sing with his wonderful voice, and he became my husband shortly after.

Group of Choir Girls and Sunday School Teachers with our priest *Above my head. Front Row L-R fourth is sister Lucy.

Front Row middle three children between angels, Francisca, Brother Tony, and Me. Representing the Miracle of Fatima

Chapter IX
Jobs and Chores

The year the twins were born, 1947, I started school. I loved school. That year, Mom had permission for me to come home at half day to help her with the babies. The first chore of the day was to hold one of them while she bathed the other. Then we'd trade and I'd feed one while she bathed the second one. Dad had made a crib for the two of them, but they'd wake each other up, so he had to make a second one. They were more like cradles, and I'd rock the twins to sleep while Mom tended to the laundry and other chores.

Harvesting of the corn was a great time. Some families traded days with other families and took turns harvesting and hauling many loads of corn to each other's houses and barns. The hauling was done with ox-carts, which looked like the old fashioned wagons in America, but instead of being pulled by horses, a pair of oxen was used to pull the heavy carts.

Corn husking was always done in the evening. That way, the women and children would pull the husks down and the men would separate the ears from all the husks. The villagers saved the corn husks, which were dried in the sun for a few days. We'd shred them and fill our mattresses with the pieces. We dried the corn ears in the oven and then we'd remove the kernels from the cobs and put them away in big barrels to be eaten during the year.

Both of our grandparents had mills in their barns. Whenever our family needed flour for baking, we knew where to go first. Their mills were built like a merry-go-round, pulled by an ox or a horse. Two large, round stones rolled over each other to grind the corn. The grain was fed under the top stone, and was turned into flour. Other times we had to take the corn to the public mill at the end of our village and/or to another village. Engines were used to run those mills.

We also had two windmills in our village. Wind permitting, we'd use them often to grind our corn.

Sometimes Mom sent my brother Joe and me, to the village of Rosais, with our bags of corn to be milled, about a two hour walk from our house. We often had to wait several hours for our turn. While there, we'd get very hungry. But, we'd remember what Mom always told us.

"Never take anything from anybody, no fruit, and no vegetable from anyone's field. And if possible, never ask for anything from others."

However, in an emergency, we knew we could ask for a piece of bread. What a great opportunity for us to test her advice.

One time we noticed that a house close to the mill had a lot of smoke coming out of the chimney. Someone had to be baking. With little brother behind me, I knocked on the door, and with great embarrassment, we told the lady our story, "We come all the way from Santo Amaro, and have been at the mill for several hours and are hungry." The lady told us to wait a minute, turned back to her kitchen and came out with an individual loaf of bread for each of us.

We didn't get home till dark, that time, but Mom had our dinner waiting for us, and we were happy kids. I learned that at times it is OK to ask for assistance when in need.

Harvesting the wheat was amazing. The men cut the wheat seed, put it in huge bundles that they carried to the one and only thrashing mill in the village. They used oxen to pull heavy wooden flats over the wheat to separate the grain from the stocks.

Wheat was very expensive. Very seldom did we eat wheat bread, except during the Holy Ghost festivals. We usually sold whatever we grew. Sometimes we worked at cultivating and harvesting for the bigger farmers in our village.

The women made straw hats for villagers from the wheat stocks, which were flattened and woven.

Because so many trees grew around the wheat fields, we were usually plagued by wild birds. In order to save the crops, we'd hang scarecrows and flags around the fields. As children, a few of us would spend hours guarding those fields, another one of the jobs we were hired to do. At times it was fun, and other times not so much fun, especially when Dad would watch us from another property on the hills above. He could tell if we were doing a good job or not. All we had to do was shake noise makers and walk up and down through the fields, with few breaks in between.

The other popular crop, at one time, was flax which turned into linen. Mom made sure she kept this custom going for several years, even after very few people grew flax. Mom didn't want us to miss the whole process. We did it more for a hobby. Going through all the steps that required us to get linen out of such plants was indeed also fascinating. After I came to America, I had the opportunity to visit a farm in Missouri and there I was so pleased to see that process still existed. We used the linen cloth for kitchen towels and to cover some of our mattresses.

Our Family also raised our own sheep, which we sheared ourselves and processed the wool to make our sweaters and socks. That process was a lot easier because we all worked on it, especially in the evening, pulling the wool pieces apart so Mom could card them and then spin the wool during the day.

I learned to spin and loved to knit and crochet the strands of wool into garments. Mom would purchase fabric dye. My most favorite sweater was red and long sleeved, tinted just for me. I loved the color red. I was so proud of that sweater. I remember going around to a couple of neighbor friends to model my new sweater. The very first thing I ever knitted was a small sweater for one of the twins.

I got bored and never finished the second one. Mom had to bail me out on that one.

New Zealand flax was very popular in our village. Dad planted many of those shrubs for two reasons. The plants made great retaining walls to prevent erosions, and the long leaves, when shredded and dried, were used to make ropes.

We also used them to weave area rugs and runners, as most kitchens had dirt floors. Those rugs and runners saved us from slipping, and kept the wood floors cleaner in the rest of the house. My sister, Madalena, was a great weaver of rugs. She spent many hours and days on her hands and knees, weaving away. Like other jobs, weaving rugs was back-breaking. Sometimes our family was hired to weave rugs for others. Sometimes we kept some rugs for ourselves.

We usually made a game out of most of our chores, but there was one chore I still cringe about when I think of it-- cultivating sweet potatoes.

Dad leased a five-acre piece of land located in the foothills. We called it *Canto*, corner. This flat parcel was delightful because of its accessibility by oxcart. We were able to load our crops right there without having to carry them to another location.

The road to this property was a place where on Sundays some people would take their walks through the most amazing hydrangeas on one side, and a small creek on the other.

In the summer time when the creek dried up, lots of white sand became exposed at the bottom, as well as enormous boulders.

On the way to the property, we'd stop to play for a while, climbing up those boulders and jumping into the sand, a great game for us who weren't capable of walking a straight line to go do our chores.

At the property, Dad would build large, raised, dirt beds where he'd plant the sweet potatoes. As soon as they grew a few feet of long stems, our job was to turn the leafy stems over, so none of the stems would grow extra roots, leaving only the main roots in the ground.

As the plants matured, they lured the worse destructive enemies possible--large larva worms, that if allowed to survive would eat all the leaves and everything else in their path. Hence the worse job created for us kids.

Armed with weapons made by Dad, a stick with a sharp nail at the end, we'd walk around the potato beds and spear our food enemies with great vengeance.

On those rare times, Mom allowed us to wear our brothers' pants. I'd plead with her. "Mom, please let me wear Tony's pants. I am so scared worms would touch my legs". And she'd say, "I don't like to see my girls wear pants. You can take them with you, and put them on over your clothes when you get there".

Thanks, Mom. You knew how to calm my fearful heart.

Mom was not a typical farmer's daughter, her two older sisters were married when she was still very young, and left her, the only girl, to help Grandmother with house chores. She rarely worked in the fields, she was a Mom at heart, and we loved knowing she was always home.

Corn Harvest in Ladeira

Oxen Cart in the Azores

Plow used to work the land pulled by horse or oxen

Ladeira: Dad cultivated some of these very steep parcels, All done by hand, accessible only by foot

Chapter X
The Joy of Reading

> "Education is what remains after one has forgotten what one has learned in school."
> Albert Einstein

We knew, through our grapevine of friends, about novels and love stories. Those were as taboo in our house as dancing and wearing make-up.

One day, an aunt of mine got a hold of a very large book titled, "O *Martir Do Golgota*," The Golgotha's Martyr. The book was about the history of Herod, the Jewish king. It was about the wars and thieves of those times, as well as the birth of Jesus, and the slaughter of thousands of innocent little boys after Jesus' birth. The book was not about religion. This book had the story of Jesus, therefore, we were allowed to read it. My aunt was good friends with Mom. She talked Mom into letting us read the book. However, we needed to find the time and the place to read such a huge volume.

We had a plan. The only light in our house at night was a three-inch kerosene lamp. We spent the evening together, either in the kitchen or in the living room in order to share the lamp. When we got a little older, my sister, Madalena, and I had been allowed to have a small bed in the living room, instead of our parent's room, giving us a little freedom. We decided to wait until everyone else was in bed. We then had the little lamp to ourselves by our bed.

Since walls of the house didn't go all the way to the ceiling, our parents could tell if we had the light on, which was not allowed in order to save on kerosene. We had a great idea. We took a medium-sized box, with the opening facing us, placed the kerosene lamp inside it, opened our book, and read silently for hours.

In order to keep silent and not be detected, we made a game of signaling to each other. When the first one of us got to the end of a page, they would tap the other with their elbow. That way the person left reading would turn the page when she got to the end. That book was full of adventure, love, and violence.

In the morning, when we got up, we'd look at each other's face and notice our nostrils were pitch black from the kerosene smoke. Before anyone else noticed, we'd clean up and go face Mom to do the chores of the day.

I often wonder if she suspected the truth, but she never questioned us, and we never confessed our sin of disobedience. The joy of reading was my most precious gift growing up in my village.

Our Kerosene Lamp

My school house, my cousin Isabel and me 1997

Chapter XI
Azorean Jobs

Dad loved being a farmer, and having his own small business. He sold the milk from his seven cows to a cheese factory. He also raised calves, sheep, and goats to sell and trade.

During 1947, Dad lost the lease on the pasture and had to give up his business. He went to work in road construction for the state. He had to travel to the end of the island and was gone during the week, leaving only the weekend to attend to whatever farming he did.

At that time, he'd been allowed a few pieces of land for crop sharing. Those orchards were only accessible by foot. Most of this land had never been cultivated, but Dad was good at clearing it and planting many types of crops. The landlords loved my dad, who surprised them with crops they would have never had otherwise. All of the neighboring land owners loved Dad as well, because he made their properties accessible by clearing trails.

As Dad traveled to the southern end of the island, he had his eye on a piece of land that stood in the middle of the island, very isolated and inaccessible. That property had been abandoned for over a hundred years. Dad saved all of his earnings and purchased this land, 12 acres of trees and shrubs.

The property was on a hill, separated on one side by a creek with large stones. When it rained, the stream formed a waterfall that spilled into the ocean a few miles away.

As we went to the property to get wood, we couldn't cross the creek because it overflowed, and we'd probably end up in the ocean along with the debris from the mountains. The stream took everything in its path, including trees and animals, because it became so strong.

Before reaching the creek, we had to walk through a forest of tall trees, under which the ground was covered with green ferns. Dad cleared a trail that meandered through the ferns. Those ferns were almost as tall as we were, and very dense. Meandering through them was magical, their aroma refreshing.

On the trees above, hundreds of pigeons made nests and we could hear their cooing, which made this part of our walk a very peaceful and memorable experience.

The process of clearing our way through our property was all accomplished by our dad's hands, with the help of a few of his older sons and daughters.

On one occasion, I saw my dad with a long rope tied to his waist, with the other end tied around a tree, which kept him from falling down into the creek, while he built a retaining wall at the bottom of the property. Thank God my brother Tony, who was four years my senior, was there. Seeing how frightened I was, he reassured me that Dad was safe.

As soon as Dad could clear a few feet of ground, he'd plant some vegetables and divide a good portion into smaller parcels, around which he'd build walls in order to prevent erosion, as the property was on a very steep hill.

Within a few years, Dad had planted over a hundred orange trees and many other fruit trees. He also built a small shack at the top of the property where we kept all our tools.

The best thing about this property was the cooking and baking of all our food in a wood burning stove. We had wood available to use because of this property. Since wood was expensive and difficult to get in those days, having our own fuel was a great asset for our family.

I'll always remember the two-hour daily round trips to our property. Most of the trips were in the early morning. Dad would wake us up at 3:00 a.m., give us fresh milk from the cow, with bread that Mom made, and out we went. We'd fetch wood and vegetables, and I'd get home just in time to go to school.

One of Dad's friends gave the boys a small donkey that had been born with a defective foot. It was meant to be a pet, but as he grew, we used him to help us bring wood, vegetables, or whatever we needed to carry to our house. We'd take turns riding the donkey. During those rides, I taught brother Lewie how to recite the Mass in Latin. We practiced for hours throughout the week on that old beaten-down gift of a donkey.

The best times for us were when we went to the property after school. We had to cross by the side of a huge volcanic crater. Around this crater were mountains and acres of land covered by black sand from that volcano. We had adult supervision to help us cross.

A few of us would run ahead, cut a lively green branch from a tree with a sickle. We'd carry it to the top of the highest point on the mountain, pretending it to be a pull cart, we'd take turns sitting on it. One would pull the cart running down the mountain, covering us all with ash from the volcano.

I can still picture the site. That place faced the ocean and I could see two of the nine islands in the distance, Pico and Faial, which are about eleven miles out.

Many times on those expeditions, I could see the small whale-hunting boats. Sometimes, there would be a monstrous black shadow being dragged behind one of them.

As a child, I felt sorry for the whales. Without these giant mammals, my family would not have oil for our lamps. We also used their bones for our tools.

In 2010, I visited the whale museum in Faial. I've witnessed firsthand videos of how the hunting was accomplished, and how the millions of pounds of flesh and bones were manufactured into the oil and tools. This ancient industry has left many wonderful memories that are deeply engraved into my soul.

Cutting up a whale in Velas San Jorge

Chapter XII
Capelinhos Volcano

1957 was a year that most immigrants from the Azores will never forget. During the month of April, the people of the central islands, Pico, Faial, and, São Jorge started to experience tremors. The priest of our village initiated what he called, *procissão de penitência*, penance processions. We carried statues of the saints in procession around the village, asking God for mercy. As a sign of penance, those who wore shoes were encouraged to walk bare footed.

One time, on my walk home from church, I heard the violent shaking of the windows of someone's house. At first I didn't know what had happened, until I saw the owners of the house run out in horror. We were pulling weeds in one of our potato fields when another quake hit. That time, we could see the ground wave up and down a long way in the distance. We ended up experiencing over 300 seismic events throughout the month of April.

To make it a more horrible experience, we were always told that thunder storms, earthquakes, and other natural disasters were punishments from God.

Each time a storm hit, our parents had us on our knees with our rosaries in hand, praying until it passed. The prayer said in part; *Jesus Nazareno, Rei dos Judeus. Livrai-nos da morte repentina*. Which means, Jesus of Nazareth, King of the Jews, deliver us from sudden death.

That prayer was just as scary as the disasters themselves. Those quakes were a constant reminder of the wrath of a very angry God.

Six months later, on September 27, 1957, a submarine volcanic eruption occurred that lasted 13 months. The eruption took place in the northern part of Faial, about eleven miles from us. At first, we could see the huge cloud of dark smoke, larger than the island itself. At other times, we could hear roaring, like thunder, and then other times we could see the red lava high above the island. We learned what was happening by telegrams sent to Velas, and each day we got more and more news and even photographs. These photographs were displayed at the local store given to the village. To this day, I still do not know who took those pictures.

Many nights we slept on our parent's bed, especially when we could hear the roaring sound and see the bright red cloud over the island that illuminated ours. After each eruption, the trembling of the ground ceased, but our nerves never calmed down. When I left São Jorge in 1959, the Volcano was still active. Over four thousand victims from Faial had to be evacuated, many to the United States. We give thanks for the efforts of the late President, John F. Kennedy, who was a Senator at that time, and we also thank the American government for its assistance.

The entire village of Capelos was destroyed. The light house was buried by ash and lava. The parish church, and all the houses were destroyed as well.

Capelinos Volcano Eruption 1957

Chapter XIII
Hard Lives Lead to America

Due to the lack of any industries, Dad's many jobs were temporary labor, mostly having to do with agriculture -- planting of the vegetables and fruits, weeding and harvesting. He also had a couple of road construction assignments. When he did, it usually meant staying away from home during the week. There were times when he was building a road in *Santo António*, to the north, and other times he was doing road work at the east end of the island.

When Dad worked on our property, he didn't earn a salary. He'd do it on weekends. As my two older brothers left home to go in the military, and to build their own lives, Dad was left with many mouths to feed, very little income, and not enough land to grow corn for bread. We had to purchase most of it, often for a very high price.

Brother Joe, at about age 15, was given the responsibility of caring for the parcel of land we crop-shared and caring for our animals. I can still picture him with two oxen pulling a huge steel plow, which he had to turn by his own strength at the end of each row -- brutal work for such a young lad.

Our village was small and filled with wheat and corn fields. The population was around 2,000 and most of the land was owned and operated by a few families. We all worked at one time or another for those landowners. They hired workers to plant, cultivate, and harvest their fields. They also hired workers to care for their animals. Most of the planting, cultivating and harvesting was accomplished by hand. Silos were built in the city of Velas, one of the two main cities of the island, and all of those crops were stored there for later exportation. We seldom shared the fruits of our hard labor.

Our island was rich in resources. We had plenty of grain and other food, such us beef, fruit, potatoes, and the famous *Queijo de São Jorge*, São Jorge cheese. However, it was more profitable to export them to the mainland. The landowners were the only ones who had communication with Portugal.

São Jorge also had plenty of ground water, but there was no one in charge of making sure it got to the various public fountains, called *chafariz*. The people of the islands had learned complacency, due to the lack of schooling and their subservient spirit. They stayed that way until the '70s and '80s. When enough returning immigrants returned to the islands with fresh ideas, they then decided to rebel against the motherland. They finally took back control of the islands creating their own local government that resembles our State system today.

I remember one time as a child being sent to one of the landowner's home with cash in my hand, begging him to sell us a bag of corn for bread. I was sent home empty handed. We knew they had the corn, but they refused to sell it to me.

As we grew older in size and in needs, most of us began to feel our parent's pain for not being able to provide even the very basic necessities. Dad worked in construction, masonry, and other hard labor jobs, and was also involved in harvesting rocks. He'd go up in the mountains, drill into the huge boulders and blow them up with dynamite. Our homes and all our buildings were built with stone. These stone structures could withstand the frequent hurricane winds. One of the churches in the neighboring village of *Urzelina* was built by my father. He also shaped bricks, with his own hands, that were used to make the cobblestone streets in many of our cities .

The other job Dad was so famous for, was to build and repair brick ovens. Every kitchen had a brick wood-burning oven. Because of the price and scarcity of wood, the ovens needed to be well insulated. Dad was a genius in this area and he traveled to many villages at night to fix those ovens. People from every village knew and loved my father, and they would marvel at his expertise and gifting. All his hard work, seven days a week, only allowed for the very basic necessities to be met -- bread and water, and little more.

Given the opportunity, Dad knew he could do better. He kept getting more and more stressed and frustrated with the situation he was in. We would have suffered hunger on top of the injustices if it was not for his hard labor. These were the days of working from the time we could walk, with so little compensation for the hard labor.

All my dad ever wanted was a little piece of land he could cultivate that would provide enough to feed his family.

One thing I wish to make clear, is that having been raised poor doesn't sadden me to this day. If anything, it has given me a survival spirit. I learned this well from my parents and my two older stronger brothers. This is the reason I developed my strong, independent spirit.

Our grandparents had been in America, and we were in constant correspondence with Mom's sister from America. Therefore, we knew we could find a better life in America, even though none of us had more than a 3rd-grade education.

The year I finished 3rd grade, the school system changed the mandatory time from 3rd to 4th grade. Immigrants from the Azores will attest that those that graduated from the 4th grade were considered more accomplished. I was fortunate to go to fourth grade.

School was an exciting time for me. My favorite subject was math. I had the multiplication tables memorized in third grade. Spelling was just as much fun. We had art work only on Saturdays. We went to school on Saturdays, mostly for half a day, which was a great time to do some coloring. We used coloring pencils. A good friend of mine would give me the broken tips of her pencils, which I'd put at the end of thin bamboo tubes. I made a full set of the six basic colors. Having a set of "real" coloring pencils was a luxury. We also had the opportunity to play hopscotch outside in the small yard of the one room school house. Hopscotch was the only form of recreation allowed.

I found a way to compensate and trade my time. I'd help some girl with her math problems and she'd help me with another subject. That simple.

We used chalk and small slates to write on and do our math problems.

I was not the best speller in my class, Ana was. I seldom misspelled words. The teacher would open a book and dictate a few paragraphs aloud. We would write down the sentences and she'd underline any error in red. Usually each error equaled a whack to the hand with a ruler. This was the only time we used paper and regular ink pens. We did that once a week in the 3rd and 4th grades. I felt left out when I saw several red marks on my friend's papers and none on mine. However, my hands never felt left out from getting a whack. The teacher liked me. She saw me as a bright child. I was afraid of her, and I never took her admiration and inspiration for granted.

Our one-room school house had a row of desks on each side, a large table at the head of the room where the teacher sat, a blackboard behind the teacher's desk, and a world map, as well as the map of Portugal on one wall. A small table sat by the entrance, decorated by a large clock and a flower vase.

My graduation day was the most memorable day of my youth, but also the saddest. The date was June 20, 1950.

Preparation for graduation was intense. We practiced our spelling, mathematics and above all, history. I wrote many essays on the kingdoms of Portugal, memorized all the king's names, learned all the rivers in Portugal, and the capitals of all the European countries.

Dad made me a stained wooden box for my graduation to carry my supplies in. Mom altered a floral dress that had come from America. She fixed my hair with two braids, tied to each other at the back with two bows, and off I went to meet the rest of my schoolmates -- Lina, Celestina, Ana, Isabel, and Isilda. Ours was an all-girl school.

We were taken to the city, *Velas*, by automobile, one of the three autos that existed in our village. This was my very first ride in a car, a shiny black, model "T" Ford. All us girls, plus the teacher and the chauffeur, were packed into the Ford like sardines.

I don't recall all the details of the exam, except that it took most of the day to complete it. I do remember the history quiz on *Pedro Alvarez Cabral*, Portuguese explorer and navigator. That was easy for me.

When I got home from the city, I went to the end of our property where I cried my heart out. In order to hide the emotional pain, which was not something we were often allowed to express. I went off on my own. I felt as if my life had just ended. I loved books and I loved to learn, but that part of my life had been cut short at ten and a half years of age.

I borrowed most of my school books, that I needed for school. We had no access to books, magazines or anything of that sort, simply because the Azores Islands were so isolated.

The one thing that I did learn at the very end of grammar school was how to tell time. Our family was like other families who didn't own a clock. However, our neighbor had a beautiful grandfather clock, that he and his wife had brought from America. Therefore, when we needed to know what time it was, we would run up to their house and look.

In the summer time, we could guess the time. All we had to do was look at our shadows. The shorter they were, the closer it was to noon. Noon was the best time of the day for us, especially when we were working in the fields. We also had the tolling of the church bells, every day at 6:00 a.m., noon, and 6:00 p.m. This was a reminder to pray, but also served as a reminder of the time of day or evening. We also would glance at the roads out yonder, and we would spot many baskets covered with white table cloths carried by women who were bringing lunch to the workers. A beautiful sight to see. This ritual meant we would be close to break time. Dad usually sent one of us home to bring back our lunch. We had no refrigeration or any other way to keep our food fresh in the working fields. Mom always had lunch ready to feed her husband and little ones.

Children of the village usually started school after their seventh birthday, except for me. Cousin Isabel was a few months older, so she'd be starting school a year ahead of me. Mom went to the director's office in Velas and received permission for me to start school the same year as Isabel, because we lived the furthest from that school. That way, we could keep each other company on the long walk to school and back.

When I began school, I was vaccinated for small pox, one of the first medical interventions I experienced. There was the time Dad took me to Velas to be checked by the pharmacist for a rash I had on my face. I was four years old. The pharmacist gave Dad some cream to rub on my face and the rash cleared up. I recall that long trip from Velas so well -- a treacherous uphill climb, and about a two-hour walk. At the same time, a lady from our village was traveling back home, and as she and Dad walked together, she turned to me and said, "Your dad should carry you on his shoulders." Dad's reply was, "She's a big girl. She's four," and that was that.

Our island had one doctor and a small medical center. I knew the doctor's name, but never had to consult him. Instead of doctors or dentists, my family used many remedies. Our garden was full of herbal medicines for every symptom. Tarragon leaves were great to clean our teeth; the only tooth brush we ever had until we came to America. Rosemary was used for tummy aches. We used citron mixed with boiled orange tree leaves for stomach indigestion. Chamomile, was a little puffy yellow flower, but with not so great an aroma. Dad used chamomile a lot. I have no idea why, but I think it was for his stomach. The aromatic leaves of lemon verbena made a great delicate tea. We used the leaves for a relaxing, calming tea. Those were but a few of our herbal medicines. However, we didn't have the sugar to add to those remedies, so we kids kept our symptoms to ourselves, as much as possible. We were very healthy kids. The only time we were all sick at the same time was when I was twelve. We all had whooping cough. I recall Dad pacing around the house with my brother Frank in his arms, and Mom with Lucy in hers. They both would convulse and we could see our parent's fearful faces at the thought of losing a child.

Lucy had been born with a heart condition. Her lips would turn purple, and her little head would shake. This wasn't diagnosed until she came to America, when she was eighteen years old.

The day after Lucy was born, my parents took her to church to be baptized. In case she died, she'd at least have a soul. After a while, she adjusted to her condition, but she always caught colds and coughed a lot. She also had bad tonsils which were often infected. We were told by some folks that she probably would get over her many sicknesses if she had her tonsils removed. We also heard that there was an organization that might help pay for having her tonsils removed. We were also told that we should take her to the hospital on the island of Terceira.

Mom and I went to Velas to the office of this organization, which was a public assistance organization we'd never heard about. When we got there, we went to a lady's office, and Mom explained to her why she and I were there.

The lady's first question was, "How many children do you have?" When Mom told her how many, the lady turned to Mom and said, "The only help we can give you is to send you home so that you can give some of those kids away. You can't afford them and we can't help you."

My mom was very quiet, shy, and loving, but her reply to the lady resonates forever in my memory. She looked at the woman and said, "Madam, it is with great difficulty that we sometimes have to give puppies, or kittens away. But my babies? They are worth way more than that." And with that, she grabbed my hand, and we calmly walked out.

On the way home, Mom could not hide her tears. As I walked with her, I had no clue what to say to her because I was just a young teen.

When she was in America, Lucy went into surgery with a defective aorta. A miracle took place. She could have died if she had gone into surgery on that little island.

She had heart surgery at Stanford Hospital in California to repair her aorta when she was in her thirties.

Ten years later the scar tissue gave way. She went to be with the Lord at age forty-six.

4th Grade Graduation
Me, Lina, Celestina, Ana, Isabel, Izilda

City of Velas

PART TWO

THE JOURNEY

Chapter XIV
Coming To America

Dad heard the Portuguese government was giving land grants in Angola, Africa, to anyone who had the ability and some tools to work the land. That was "music" to Dad's ears. He mentioned it to Mom, but right away she rejected the idea, the main reason being that her parents were getting older and she was the only daughter around, thus the one responsible to care for them in their late years.

Mom was a very devout Catholic. The last thing she cared about was monetary success. The "rich" were given a bad reputation by the church, maybe for a good reason, but to become one of them was not something she aspired to. Besides, she believed in carrying whatever cross came her way. She was at peace with her very poor existence but Dad was not.

However, he used to tell Mom that there was a quote in the Bible that said. "Give me your hand and I will rescue you." Dad was very faithful and he believed that God would help anyone, providing they did their part.

One day, we were told that the photo of my younger sister, Jacinta, was on display in a photographer's window in the city of Velas. A couple of us kids went to investigate and found that Dad had taken three of my siblings, one at a time, to have their photos taken in order to get our passports to go to Africa. He gave the photographer permission to display Jacinta's photo. Back we went to face Mom with the truth. Dad refused to accept Mom's no for an answer. He insisted and he was determined to take his family to a place where he could feed and care for them. Africa was the place for this goal of his. Mom was a wise woman and a great wife. She thought of a compromise. She agreed to leave the island, but not to go to Africa. The compromise was to go to her country of birth -- America.

Mom's brother was living with Grandfather when her mother passed away. He was able to care for Grandfather which allowed our family the option to leave.

Between Africa and America discussions, word got around that our family was planning to leave to go to America. Many families had already left, including some neighbors and close friends.

I was on my way to church during this time of my life and was stopped by my uncle's friend, John Cabral. He was ten years my senior and a very good looking young man. John stopped me and we had a conversation on that road. He told me that his parents were planning to send a lady to our village to marry him. This marriage would be on paper only in order for him to immigrate and be with his parents in America. John then told me that if I would agree to marry him, he'd marry me in the church and not just on paper. He'd also pay my mother to help pay for some of the costs of getting her citizenship papers.

I was seventeen and I was desperate to either go to a convent or anywhere else. I just wanted the chance to get an education and a better life, free from so much poverty.

I was interested in John's proposal and my parents were very pleased. The reason they were pleased was this. I had just broken up with my first boyfriend and they feared I may not take settling down again seriously. There was a phrase I heard often growing up. "The sooner they're taken ownership of, the better." Parents believed that to avoid the risk of us girls going astray and giving the family a bad name, young girls needed to get married at a young age.

We immediately wrote to the American Embassy. We needed to find out if getting married would cause the loss of my citizenship. Part of the immigration laws were written to declare that if a person was born to an American citizen, like I was to my mom, that child was a citizen by birth. As soon as we received the answer we were expecting to hear, I married John Cabral, six months later, on July 30, 1958.

We had a very small wedding without guests, just the immediate family. Mom and John's sister made me a white dress, and we borrowed a veil. We were married in a small chapel at the end of the road that led to my parent's house.

The reception was in the early afternoon. A special chicken dinner was the wedding feast with chickens from our parent's yard. John's sister, Maria, made a cute cake, decorated with what looked like pearls.

We set a table in my parent's living room, which overlooked the islands of Pico and Faial.

Gazing across at Pico's harbor, we could see the very well-known Portuguese ship, *Carvalho Araújo*, whose next stop within a couple of hours would be to pick up passengers at the Velas Port. Those passengers, would be John, me, and my mom. We knew we would be travelling to the big Island of São Miguel to the American consulate, in order to present our required paperwork to bring our families to America. Even though Mom and I were American citizens, and had American passports, we knew to expect the barrage of paperwork to come.

The first time I saw the ship up close was the following day in Velas. It was a majestic structure in comparison to the fishing and whaling boats we often saw. Carvalho Araujo held around 400 passengers.

The form of communication between the people of the islands and the rest of the world was by mail. The islands were not too far apart and only one ship made the rounds once a month, the Carvalho Araújo. The ship would miss a round if the weather was bad and we would have to wait another month.

The arrival and departing of the famous Carvalho was one of the major events of the islands. Imports and exports of people's goods, animals, and food was conducted on the day the ship arrived. A great event for everyone was to go to the main ports of our Islands and watch the activity and interaction with the merchants. Those events will be forever engraved in the minds and hearts of the immigrants who had the chance to witness this first hand in the Azores.

The famous Portuguese music band, O Tributo, won first prize in Europe one year, for their rendition of "É Dia De São Vapor," It's Saint Ship Day, written and sung by António Severino about the Carvalho Araújo.

The saddest days on our island was when someone was leaving us and we had to say our good byes.. Most often, they were our men leaving for the military. The tradition was to go down to the dock and personally say our good byes. The passengers could see the waving of handkerchiefs for miles after the ship left the port.

To keep the tradition, some of my friends went to the dock to say their good byes on the day we left to go to São Miguel. Some of my friends, including the cousins who could not make it to the dock, stood in one friend's yard that faced the ocean. They took bed sheets to wave goodbye to us, just to make sure we could see them. I still remember my tears, good byes were so emotional for us who had such limited communication opportunities, no cell phones, not even house phones.

The dock was too small for such a large ship, so we had to take small boats out a good distance and climb up the ship's ladder. I loved the adventure, and the opportunity to finally see the island from a distance.

Mom and I slept on small bunks on the port side of the ship, and John bunked with the men on the starboard side. I don't know if accommodations for couples were available, but if they had any, we didn't have them.

We sailed all night plus the entire next day. I don't recall the meals, but I do remember watching the dolphins follow us, jumping and playing in such a huge pool of blue water.

I knew very little about John. He had lived on the island of Terceira, and had worked there on the American Air Force base for a few years. However, in a small village, everyone knows everyone else's history.

John's parents had gone to America at separate times, when they were teenagers. They met each other in the states, married, and had two children, Isabel and William. They then returned to São Jorge, and had five more children. Isabel and William returned back to America in their teenage years. Several years later, Isabel sponsored a younger brother and sister, along with her parents, and these few went to live in America at Isabel and her husband Tony Silva's dairy farm in San Jose, California.

When we arrived in São Miguel, our travel agent met us in his automobile and took us to a small house that rented rooms by the day.

We stayed there for about one week.

We spent most of our daily time at the American embassy. Mom and I found an opportunity to visit the well-known cathedral of *Santo Cristo*, and we also walked around admiring the beautiful window displays in the nearby shops. Some of those displays had the most beautiful fabrics I had ever seen. We never went in. We just admired the beauty of it all.

John would go down to one of the pubs and have a beer and talk to the other guys and just hang out and relax.

São Miguel island has a beautiful city, *Ponta Delgada*, the only big city I had first been to. What an amazing experience to see a city. Going to the nearest plaza and counting the parked automobiles was such a treat. I recall counting up to forty automobiles. This was incredible and exciting to a country girl.

We returned to São Jorge one week later and lived at John's parent's house. We returned with a big list of requirements from the America Embassy. We also borrowed more money to pay all these requirements. We also had to get affidavits from the United States. We needed someone who would be responsible for us for one year. We had to have job offers with salary for all the adults that were arriving to their new dream. We also had to have chest X-rays, and every type of vaccine imaginable at that time to the medical community.

Everything we had in Portuguese had to be translated into English.

Six months later, in January 1959, John and I decided to go back to São Miguel. We thought that if we showed up in person, we'd get our answers sooner than later. All we accomplished was giving the travel agent more money, and we never saw any progress.

We went through this mundane process for three months. Since I had an American passport, I was allowed to go to America any time. John's sister was ready to go with her husband to the United States. John decided to send me with them. On April of 1959, the three of us flew on a small plane to the international airport on the island of Santa Maria. From this island, we took a TWA propeller flight direct to the state of New York. It was a ten-hour flight.

World War II had ended when I was very young. The stories of war were engraved in our minds, as well as the effects of "rationing of commodities." We continued to see big war ships stretched out between the islands after the war was over. The airport of Terceira, north of São Jorge had become an American Air Force base, which served as a refueling spot for the war planes and war ships. The war between the world and the roaring of the airplanes overhead was an ugly reminder of evil in this world. Every time American planes flew over our island, they gave me a terrifying experience and a reminder of what hatred can do to mankind.

I can still recall how I felt on the flight from Santa Maria to New York. All I could do was shake in complete shock that I was now in one of those planes. Sometimes the airplane would climb, other times it would drop for a while. My experience on this air flight was very traumatic for me and I remained traumatized many years later.

As we were finally approaching New York, the captain told us to look out the window to see the Statue of Liberty. It'd be a few years before I learned about that famous Statue, and another several years later before I had the pleasure of visiting this land mark monument. She still holds many fond memories for all Americans today.

After landing at Idlewild airport in New York, I asked myself, "How could those stairs at the airport take people up and down without their feet moving?" Doors opened and closed without us touching them. This was all awe-inspiring to me. There were people everywhere, coming and going from every direction.

A gentleman then guided us to the gate for our flight to San Francisco.

From New York to San Francisco was another 12-hour flight. Someone aboard the plane gave me a sedative and I slept for the most part of that trip.

When we finally arrived in San Francisco, we got off the plane and John's parents, his sister Isabel, and her husband Tony Silva greeted us. They then took us to their dairy farm in San Jose where we resided at John's parent's house on this little ranch.

The ride from San Francisco to San Jose was also amazing. I had never seen so many lights in my entire life. Every inch of the road was lined with them -- lights high on posts, lights passing us by, lights of all different colors. Our skies in the Azores were beautiful with millions of stars everywhere. The lights of San Francisco were also a wonderful sight to experience.

As soon as I arrived in San Jose, the family consulted a travel agent to assist me in my new home. Mr. Jack Peixoto was an honorable man. He notified us that our required immigration papers for the United States had never been received from either John or me. My next part of this new journey was to start the petition of bringing my husband to America. This took another three months of hard work and time. John finally arrived in San Francisco in July 1959, right before our first wedding anniversary.

Mom and Dad were having the same difficulties with immigration documentation. I feared they'd be discouraged and give up trying to come to America. John and I had made it through this grueling process and that gave my parents the motivation needed to keep on filling out all of their paperwork.

In October of that same year, Mom, Dad, and eight of my siblings, ages 6 to 17, arrived at the San Francisco International Airport. My two older brothers had to wait a few more years before they were allowed to come to the states. Tony, who was still single, came two years after our parents. John, came six years later with his wife and their five small children.

We were now finally all together in America. How fortunate our family was to be on the same continent, in the same country, and the same state.

We were truly blessed.

Carvalho Araujo

My Wedding Day
I was 18
John was 28

Chapter XV
Our First Jobs in America

> *"Opportunity is missed by most because it is dressed in overalls and looks like work"*
> Thomas Edison

John was hired by his sister and brother-in-law, to work at their dairy farm. We lived on the farm in one of their houses, with two bedrooms and one bath.

The Silva's had been executors for an elder gentleman's will. He was a friend of theirs who had recently passed away. We were given the opportunity to purchase all the furniture in this gentleman's house,. This included all appliances and all of the dishes. We had a nice little house on the farm and fully furnished. John had a hard job but it was a paid job. His shifts went from two a.m. to late morning, and then again at two p.m. till evening. This shift was for all seven days of the week.

Life on the dairy farm was very isolated. We didn't drive, nor did we have time to go anywhere. I marveled at the immense herd of cows coming to the barn twice a day to have their milk taken with machines, which in turn ran through glass pipes into enormous tanks. The milk was carried by huge trucks out of the farm and into oblivion to awaiting cheese factories. I loved visiting the cows but I started getting home sick. I missed my little brothers and sisters, and all of my girlfriends. I also missed walking to church. There were many days I would hear the airplanes fly over the farm. I had the same thought that I had in the little chapel on my wedding day. This thought would creep into my head, "Am I ever going to get out of this?" I was wishing that one of those airplanes would sweep me up and carry me back home. I'd be willing to hang on to its wings, as long as I could go home.

John's father, who was in his seventies and still working at the dairy, was the most loving man on earth. In the afternoons, when he was free, he'd take me out to his porch and we'd sit and count cars coming out of the IBM plant at the end of Downer Avenue, which is now Blossom

Road. When we'd get to three hundred, we'd quit and laugh. We knew that not one single person in São Jorge would believe us, even if we told them. In fact, I doubt if we could even fit three hundred cars on our island.

My father-in-law and I would also watch cartoons and comedy shows together. My favorites were The Three Stooges, and Laurel and Hardy. One did not have to know much English to understand most of what was going on . John's dad did not understand English either, but we sure laughed a lot together on those precious times.

One evening, after dinner at John's parents, I got up from the dinner table and started to clear the dishes. I took a large pot, filled it with water, and set it on the stove. I then turned the fire on. John's mother asked me what I was doing. Filled with pride for my housewife abilities, I told her I was heating the water to wash the dishes. In a nice and gentle way, she walked me over to the sink and showed me how on "the other side of the faucet" the water was already hot. Instead of feeling mortified and deflated, I thought to myself, only in America can we witness such a miracle.

The next time John's sister went grocery shopping, I also went along. To my surprise, we did not need to bring our own containers or bags to carry the groceries back home. I was amazed that the groceries, such as, sugar, flour, spices and all others came in their own boxes and bags. They also had recipes and pictures printed on them. I may not have been able to understand the writing on them, but this gave me another opportunity to learn and to read. Learning was always available at every moment around me. It saddens me to this day to think how many gifts we Americans take for granted.

Two years later, after John and I paid our debt to his parents we'd incurred with our trip and paperwork, we bought our first automobile, a used 1958 yellow Pontiac. My parents were living in Gilroy, and we had the opportunity to visit them there.

By this time, another brother-in-law of John's was working for a lumber company. His wife worked at Levi Strauss and Company sewing Levi jeans. They got jobs for both of us in the respective companies. We moved into a duplex in the city of Santa Clara. Santa Clara was Mom's birthplace.

John's employer was only a couple of miles from home. My job was in downtown San Jose. I took the bus to work every day with other ladies from the Azores. We became friends on that bus and enjoyed working together.

I loved my job at Levi'. It was the most physical, challenging job of my life -- sewing jeans on an industrial-fast machine. Each department did one part of the pants. My job was putting together the side seams and inseams.

The industrial sewing machines were humongous and intimidating. Each carton held 100 pair of jeans. The average ticket for a carton was $3.50. I tried to meet my goal each day. The goal was four cartons a day. I tried my best daily. There were many days that I didn't reach the quota.

We were paid by piece work. The faster we could sew, the more money we made, and seldom was it more than minimum wage.

I was very grateful for my job. Living in town, seeing and talking to different people every day, walking and/or taking a bus to any store, and especially walking to church, were the greatest experiences of my life. John and I bought a used sewing machine. We bought nice clothes from the Goodwill store in town, and I used the machine to alter and make clothes. We even bought John a nice brown suit. This was the best suit he had for many years of his life. I altered the pants for him. He loved it and looked great in his new suit.

I always assumed that I would get pregnant sooner or later. I still recall telling my Mom that I missed having a baby of my own. Her reaction to me was, "Haven't you had enough?" I was raised with babies all my life. Mom gave us a new one every other year and always made sure we never lacked in the baby industry. When Mom had a new child, it sometimes felt like the one born prior to the new baby was now rejected. I was sorry for that little brother or sister who was not getting the attention they used to get. I'd make sure to care for that rejected one by giving him or her all the love and attention I could. Why wouldn't I want one of my very own?

Shortly after my parents arrived, Dad started working at a ranch, and Mom and the rest of the siblings worked in the fields gathering cucumbers. In about a years time, they had paid the $5,000 debt that they had incurred. The debt had accrued due to a very high interest rate. This now freed them to register the six younger ones into a private school, Saint Mary's Catholic School in Gilroy.

Five years after my marriage, and with much prayer, I got pregnant. My first child, John Paul Cabral, was born on January 30, 1963, a few months before our 5th wedding anniversary.

Much to my broken heart, I had to go back to work three months after John Paul's birth. John was working for minimal wages, and we could not make it on his income. However, we knew a darling Portuguese family right around the corner and they cared for my son. Fifteen months later, we had our first daughter, Bernadette. She was born on May 15, 1964.

Our landlords were of Portuguese descent, and their daughter was a realtor. We needed a bigger place to live. With careful counseling, and the small savings we had put away, she showed us a 900 square foot cute little house.

Mom and Dad, and all the kids, were living in Santa Clara. Next to the house we bought was another one, a little larger, probably 1200 square feet, for sale. My parents purchased it. Dad made a gate between the fences that divided the two properties. It was great to live by my parents, I never had to hire baby sitters again, and the kids loved their grandparents. Sometimes I'd give Mom a little money for helping me. I found out later she saved most of it, and when she had enough she bought a swing set for our yard. In 1966, John and I were gifted with another beautiful child. Lucinda. She was born October 8, 1966. From that time on, I no longer felt able to work full time. I had three kids, and I felt that I was continuing to put that extra burden on my folks. I worked at different canneries during the next few summers, cleaned a few houses, and took in sewing and ironing jobs. I even worked at the Saint Claire's Church washing laundry and linens, to supplement our income.

Dad had suffered from osteoarthritis, most of his life much like his father before him. I've always remembered, *Avô Palhaça*, grandfather clown. Grandfather used two long canes as crutches to walk from his house to his gate, where he'd spend all day greeting anyone and everyone who went by. He, like Dad, loved people. Both of them were extroverts. Mom's family were mostly introverts. Dad never saw his father again, after Dad left for America, but he did go back and visit, 20 years later, and had a chance to see all his living brothers and sisters --
Maria, Ana, Antonio, João, Mariana and Joaquin.

In 1983, Dad went back one more final time. This time his two sons, Lewie and Joe, went with him.

Dad's poor health forced him to quit working before he was sixty. The pain in his knees, and later on in his hips, was excruciating at times. He lost both of his hip and knee joints. After several consultations with doctors, both parties decided that surgery was out of the question. He learned to walk bending only from the waist, and after several years, the pain had subsided.

Dad's house was on the corner of Di Giulio and Avila Avenue in

Santa Clara. They lived on Avila. We lived on Di Giulio. The area was light industrial, with several office and manufacturing buildings. Di Giulio had lots of traffic, including foot traffic during commute hours. People walking by often stopped to admire Dad's garden. The metal fence that went around the yard was covered with beautiful passion fruit vines and their variegated flowers and purple fruits. Several orange trees lined one side of the property. Roses, asters, and many other varieties of annuals and perennials were always on display. Even into his 80s, Dad would volunteer to prune some of the neighbor's roses and shrubs.

My brother Joe and his wife, Leonor, would often take Dad to their farm in Oakley, and Dad would prune, plant, and weed to his heart's content. His farming expertise shone through. They also took Dad and Mom on a trip across the United States to visit our brother Tony, who lived in Florida with his wife, Nina, and their two children, Lee and Charlene. Dad collected postcards from every state they stopped in.

He spent hours showing us the beauty of Arizona's red mountains, the immense orange groves of Florida, and the vast beautiful land that America possessed.

He absolutely loved seeing so much of America.

My brothers and sisters in Gilroy 1959

First Year in U.S. 1959

Chapter XVI
Dreams Come True

One day, in 1963, while watching television, and while my baby boy, John Paul, was learning to crawl on our small living room floor, I read an advertisement in the TV Guide Magazine about finishing high school at home. I filled out the application and received my first book of lessons. The correspondence school was called National Schools, located in Los Angeles. I was so thankful the first course was in English vocabulary and grammar.

My siblings who lived next door with my mom and dad, were in high school at that time. I had help from them. I shed many tears in the process of learning the English language. I fell asleep many nights with a book by my side. The thought of quitting never crossed my mind.

Some courses, like science, math, world literature, and American literature were more difficult than others. Even though they were a lot of work, they were also very fascinating to me. American history was my favorite subject. I still chuckle when I think of how I felt when I read about the Pilgrims arriving in America. Having lived most of my childhood in São Jorge, Azores, I had a lot in common with these pilgrims. We grew our own corn, lived in houses with dirt floors, used wood or animal skins for shoes and sandals, just as they did 200 years ago. I took six years to complete all of my studies.

In July 1969, I received my high school diploma. I looked outside on Avila Street and there was my boy riding his bicycle, training wheels off. He had come a long way, but so had I. Not many adult immigrants who had only a 4th grade education could achieve what I just achieved. I just felt so blessed to be here and have these opportunities.

Brother Lewie wrote a small story in the Santa Clara newspaper, which one of my employers at Gangi Bros. Packing Co. noticed. He immediately sent me to take a course in quality control. I took the course and passing it moved me from the sorting lines to the lab, where I worked for the next two years. One day, I got on my son's bike and rode it to pick up my paycheck. I was approached by the owners that day. They offered me a full time job in the accounting department. My youngest, Lucinda, was entering kindergarten at this time, October of 1971.

The timing was perfect.

I always wanted to be a bookkeeper. Two of my elective courses had been in accounting. To be an accountant seemed like a big dream to keep my heart smiling. I knew all of the office workers at Gangi Bros. I'd done sewing and ironing for a few of them. They put in a good word for me and I was hired in the bookkeeping office of Gangi Bros. I was surprised and so grateful. I had the best working partners, supervisors, and friends. Gangi Bros., a family owned and operated enterprise, became for most of us, one big happy family.

We worked long hours during the summer months which was the peak season to produce the various tomato products. God bless the Gangi family. I will never forget them as long as I live.

My long hours were compensated with a bonus at the end of the season, which meant I could now send the kids to a private school. Saint Clare's Church and school was down the road from where we lived. Mom used to go to Mass every morning. She'd walk the kids to school, then meet them after school and walk them home.

When I look back, I think of how I didn't have to take the children grocery shopping or on mundane errands, and how they never had to miss their naps because my mom was there to watch them. I was so blessed that the kids loved my parents and had the chance to grow up knowing all their visiting cousins. Every time one of my siblings came to see our parents, there were cousins galore to play with. Dad was always home planting flowers or trees, or doing some needed painting around the house. He even cemented a sidewalk all around our house so his grandchildren could ride their tricycles. He was always willing to help with the chores. For example, I didn't own a dryer for a long time. I'd put the clothes basket outside and Dad would hang the clothes on the line to dry and he often helped fold them as well.

When my children got a little older, we needed more room, so we sold our house and purchased a bigger one in Santa Clara on Bray Avenue. The kids continued to see Mom every day in church. Sometimes they'd go to her house after school. Other times they'd go home and play with all the neighbor friends after helping with their daily chores.

CALIFORNIA

Valley Living

Mother of 3 Earns Degree, To Take Business Course

Earning a high school diploma is harder for some people than others.

For Mary M. Cabral, 1031 DiGiulio Ave., it has been an especially "hard road but was worth every step."

Mary came to this country from Azores, Portugal in April, 1959. Prior to her marriage in Portugal, she had received only four years of grammar school education.

After arriving in the United States, she attended adult education classes in English at Woodrow Wilson School in San Jose and later at Santa Clara High School.

"Then, I enrolled in a correspondence course with National Schools in Los Angeles and, took one subject at a time, beginning with English," she related.

July 5, the hard work was over and Mrs. Cabral was graduated from the school with a high school diploma.

Now comes the challenge of college work, because Mary has decided to take business courses at De Anza College this fall. She eventually wishes to do bookkeeping and other secretarial work in an office.

When not studying and caring for her three children, aged 3, 5, and 6, Mary has been working as a housekeeper for the University of Santa Clara and as a summer employe at Duffy Motts.

For fun and relaxation, she likes to sew.

Mary's husband John works at Larson Ladder Co. in Santa Clara.

Not the only ambitious member of her family, Mary has three brothers—Manuel, Frank and Lewis—who are recent graduates from Santa Clara High School. Lewis is currently studying for the priesthood at Loyola Jesuit University in Los Angeles, Frank is serving with the Marines in Vietnam and Manuel recently returned from the war zone.

Mrs. Cabral is one of 11 children of Mr. and Mrs. Manuel Dias, also former residents of The Azores who now live in Santa Clara. Five of the Dias youngsters are now married and live in this area.

MARY M. CABRAL
... Earns Diploma

1969 Family
John, Me, Lucinda, Johnny, and Bernadette

Chapter XVII
Learning From My Children

One morning, as we were getting ready to leave for the day, Nicky, our collie-shepherd mix dog got excited, running around, sniffing at the refrigerator. The first thing we thought was she must be looking for some toy.

To our surprise, she was trying to chase a mouse that had crawled under the refrigerator. As I tried to scoot the mouse out with a broom, it ran into the garage. I grabbed some baseball bats, gave one to each child, and proceeded to look for the mouse in order to get rid of it. As the mouse ran behind a box, I grabbed one of the bats, and in the blink of an eye, I sent it to eternity.

I was proud of my fast reactions, until the three kids started to cry, "How could you take a little life?" I didn't think much about it. However, seeing the kids so upset made me upset, too.

When I got to work, I shared the incident with my fellow workers, Rita and Patti, who felt the kids' pain, and lectured me. I tried to explain that during part of my life in the country, I had to live with critters that did a great deal of damage to our food supply.

I then told the kids the following two stories. The first story is when my sister Madalena, who was working in the field, had just sat down to take a break, when she started to scream and grab the bandana off of her head. A mouse had crawled inside her sweater all the way to the top of the back of her neck. Of course, I made sure it had a short life span. I really, really, made sure of that.

The second story is a little more interesting. When we'd get a loaf of bread from the long board, a board Dad had hung from the kitchen ceiling to keep the loaves from bugs and critters, we'd find a perfect round hole in the middle of one, chewed by little mice teeth. Mom would scrape around the hole and with a smile she'd say, "At least we know where its mouth had been." This caused me to shiver as I also thought about the feet and tail of this little thief.

After telling my children these experiences, I'm not sure they were interested in hearing my stories or even if they wanted to talk to me ever again. The incident reminded me that they lived in a much different environment than where I was raised. Looking at their sad faces, I needed to realize that even mice have a right to live in America as well.

As the saying goes, "You can take the girl out of the country, but you can't take the country out of the girl."

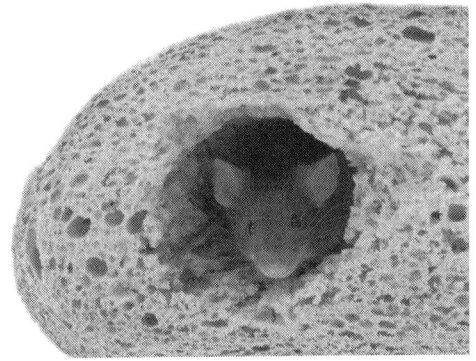

Chapter XVIII
Active Children

When my children were still very young, before their teens, I asked their dad to please teach them to read music. I was hoping that someday they would play a musical instrument so they could be in the school band, just like their dad had done for so many years as a young man. He had played the trombone in a marching band back home. This is one of the few opportunities I had to listen to music. I loved music so much and growing up there were no radios. I never heard of a radio before I arrived in America.

At first, when I mentioned the kids taking music lessons, he was against the idea, but I kept insisting that it would be a great gift to pass down to his son and daughters. After a while, he mentioned my idea to some of his friends at work. One of these friends had also played in a band. Together, the two men decided to start a children's music class at the Portuguese Hall down the street. They then formed a band with about 40 members from all around the Bay Area, called the Santa Clara Portuguese Band.

Musicians came from as far as Watsonville California, which is a city about fifty miles away from Santa Clara. The band leader was from Newark. Most of the musicians were immigrants from the different Islands of the Azores. They, like John, had played in their respective bands of their villages, and were willing to travel, not just for band practice held every Saturday, but to perform and march in other cities and towns all over Northern California.

John Paul played the trumpet and Bernadette played the clarinet. They marched and played at many Portuguese festivals.

I didn't want my children to miss out on the opportunities available to them. Lucinda was not interested in band. She was interested in the piano. Therefore, she and I took lessons for a year.

Later on, the youngsters joined the Luso American Fraternal Federation, an organization that creates opportunities for children to earn college scholarships, and to compete in folkloric dancing in California. John and I travelled with them, and had a lot of fun, especially during their annual conventions. These conventions took us to San Diego, Disneyland, and many other beautiful cities.

Chapter XIX
Road to Freedom

> *"I have been all things unholy,*
> *if God can work through me, He*
> *can work through anyone."*
> Francis of Assisi

I was married now for 20 years, with three beautiful healthy children, a good job, a nice house. Why was this not enough? Why couldn't I bear my cross and live with what was dealt to me? I realized I had so many questions, and so few answers. My honest answer was, that after 20 years of marriage with John, he had never changed, but I did. I wanted to be the traditional wife. I loved being a homemaker, and I still do. I love to cook and sew, and keep a nice home. I love caring for a man, like most women, but I also realized I was to be valued as a person, not as someone's possession. I had likes and dislikes. I loved people. I had desires to continue my education. I wanted to learn how to swim, play golf, how to dance, to play music, and just to be able to talk and laugh with a friend. To John, all of that was taboo. These simple things John did not allow. These restrictions had been part of my upbringing. I was in America now. I wanted more.

I knew that divorcing John would be a difficult act against the Catholic faith. If I would go through with it, I would never be able to remarry or to participate in any sacrament like the Eucharist. Besides, I knew the pain I would cause my parents, especially my dad. Two of their sons had divorced, but my parents had different expectations for their daughters.

Coming to America, learning the American value system, the creation of a system that believes all human beings have rights, and that those rights were given to us by God, is the best and the worst for an immigrant girl.

Why? Because even though I had come from a very controlled society in the Azores, living in a free society created a tremendous struggle for me, between wanting to believe in the old system, and wanting to embrace the new.

One October day, in 1978, and with all the courage I could muster, I went to visit Dad and took him for a short walk by his house. I made the announcement that the family would have another divorce.

He turned to me and said, "As far as I'm concerned, there was never matrimony between you and John." All my worry was for nothing. I can't believe how naive I had been for so many years.

At the end of the sidewalk, my mom stood waiting and praying for us with her rosary in hand. Divorce had to be the dirtiest word in the vocabulary of a traditional Catholic family. It sure was in my family.

Mom would tell me how much she prayed for me. The things she and Dad feared the most, was ingrained in their culture, was to maintain a good family name, and never to do anything that would diminish that. Sometimes I wonder if the culture I was in believed more in appearances, than in what was going on behind closed doors. What is more important? Looking good or being truly good from the heart. But I'm not the judge. I struggled with it for too long, and the truth set me free.

Freedom is never free, but it is worth the cost one has to take to attain it. I needed release from my prison. We create our own prisons that we need release from and we allow others to place us into prisons as well. What was my prison. Could it be my childhood upbringing watching my mother as a young girl? Could parents beliefs impact their children's psyche even to their adult age?

Mother had been beaten down by a religious system that put no value on the human being. She truly believed that anything that was pleasure was a sin, especially anything that had to do with vanity.

To make matters worse, Mom also suffered from anxiety and depression from a young age, which made some days very sad as she'd spend days in bed.

We'd pray many rosaries and novenas for God to heal her, but we had no understanding of her sad days.

When I was eleven years old, I was invited to one of the Holy Ghost festivals. Mom had received some clothes from America, and in the box was the most colorful, floral dress I had ever seen. On a white background, the vivid pinks, royal blues, greens, purples, and yellows were amazing. But, there was a problem with it. The dress had short sleeves, and even though she needed to shorten the dress, there was not enough fabric to lengthen the sleeves

I was mortified when Mom took some white fabric and made long sleeves for the dress, using a little strip from the bottom to make cuffs. I knew I was going to be teased by the other girls. By now I had seen that other girls my age were allowed to wear short sleeves, cut and curl their hair, and even have their hems above the knee, and I wanted to be like the rest.

To my surprise, the old parish priest, passed by me and said, "Maria, what a beautiful dress you have." It didn't help. I would have rather stayed home.

Mom also took the message of the Miracle of Fátima, seriously. This is a belief where the blessed virgin appeared to three children in Fatima, Portugal, in 1917, and the message for the world was *virtude*, virtue, modest dressing, and for women to cover their heads with a veil or bandana for church.

Our parish priest had made an announcement in church one Sunday, that if any woman approached the communion rail while wearing lipstick, nail polish, and/or if any person had gone to a dance on Saturday night, he would pass them by and not give them communion. With that warning in mind, not a sane person would want to be embarrassed in public.

Mom lived by what the priest said, period. Back then, priests had all the power. First of all, they were the only ones who had a formal education, which equated to being smart, intelligent, and worthy of all the power and respect from everyone. After all, they were also God's ambassadors, and no one wants to mess with God.

We were taught to always treat others, especially older people, with respect. We never called anyone by their first name, we always said *Tio*, uncle, for the men, and *Tia*, aunt, for ladies. In the Azores, very few were called, *senhores*, or *senhoras*, only those in the high society.

I'm certain that the question of, "Why did some couples have so many babies, when they were so poor," was in many minds. The answer. Religion. Not only did the marriage vows contain the usual Honor and Obey, they also contained, "Do you vow to have as many children as God wants to give you?" Birth control was not only unavailable, but was also forbidden by the church. Worse yet, a Catholic couple had to confess to the priest if they avoided child conception.

Padre Rolim was a missionary who went around the islands preaching the fires of hell. As he put it, each birth a couple avoided would be turned into tongues of fire waiting for those Moms in hell. Mom used to tell us that during the year Padre Rolim spent preaching in the Azores. The result was that several women close to menopause age, were still conceiving.

I share all these beliefs to show that these deep rooted beliefs can affect the choices we make in this life, and even hinder our personal growth. Even to the point of staying unhappy in our created prisons. We are in prison in relationships, addictions, bad habits, and any other type of control, which Our Heavenly Father calls sin, because it keeps His children from being the best they can be and receiving all of His unconditional Love. "He whom the Son sets free is free indeed!" John 8:36

Many years later, in the U.S., a missionary would periodically visit Dad. When he found out Dad did not speak English, he gave my dad a Bible written in Portuguese. Through the years, Dad read that Bible over and over.

Once, on the way back from a doctor's appointment, sitting in the back seat of my car, Dad made a comment which made me laugh. He said, "There's no place in the Bible that says one must have ten children in order to be saved." He was in his 80's. The Apostle Paul wrote to the people of Galatia in Chapter 5 verse 1: It is for freedom that Christ has set us free. Stand firm, then, and do not let yourselves be burdened again by a yoke of slavery.

Looking back at the bulls of the Azores and seeing them yoked together and plowing a field reveals this truth further. The bull is yoked to the other bull. Wherever one wants to go the other must go. What do we yoke ourselves to? Jesus said, "Take my yoke upon you for my burden is light." If we walk in His unconditional love, the other yokes have no place in our lives and He removes them from our lives.

Can anyone truly say, "I have tasted that type of Freedom?"

Chapter XX
Taste of Freedom

"In the end, it's not the years that count.
It's the life in your years."
Abraham Lincoln

As I continue to grow as a person, I realize more and more that events in our lives are not always orchestrated by us. Even though we try to manage our lives the best way we can, we're not always in control. After my divorce, like any other family, finances didn't come easy. With my children still in private school, the four of us had an enormous adjustment to make.

We continued to live in our house on Bray Ave. in Santa Clara. I had to pay off one half of the equity to my ex-husband by refinancing the house, which caused the mortgage to triple.

John had a better attorney than I did. The lawyer didn't take into account the fact that now as a single parent I had full responsibility for three children.

On the day the divorce was finalized, I was ordered to pay half of the home equity to John, or to put the house on the market within thirty days. A few days later, I dropped the children off at the Vieira's home in Santa Clara for Luso dance practice. Mr. and Mrs. Vieira approached me as they noticed something was wrong and that I had been crying. I told them my dilemma about the house.

Before I left, Mr. Albert Vieira asked me to stop by his office in the morning. The next day, before work, I stopped by his office, per his request. When I walked in, he asked for the amount that I needed to pay. I told him the quantity was $35,000. He wrote a check for that amount and said, "Have your children deliver this to their dad."

Before I accepted the check I said, "Mr. Vieira, first let me write you a promissory note. I have the forms in my car." He stopped me and said, "I've known your father, an honorable man, and I know most of your family. With people like you, I need no documents." With that, he walked me to the door.

Forty-five days later, I closed the new loan on the house. When I went to pay the money back to Mr. Vieira, he would not take a cent of interest.

Mr. Albert Vieira has now gone to be with the Lord. His generosity was known in the Portuguese community, and those who knew him will never forget him.

The children had part-time jobs to help with groceries and home maintenance costs. My full-time job paid well, and offered medical and some dental care. However, I had to quit the job of selling Real Estate for the last four years in order to be around my three teenagers on weekends and evenings.

My children were very active -- junior theater, sports, music, dancing. I will always miss those times, for there was never a dull moment with the house full of three teenagers and their many friends. Their college was put on hold. John Paul joined the Marine Corps, in San Diego, which began the empty nest phase of my family.

The year of my divorce, friends of mine gave the children and me the opportunity to share the expense of renting a condo in Lake Tahoe. I packed our suitcases and the four of us were off with no idea of what we were getting into.

We'd never experienced the snow before. Getting away for a while sounded like a wonderful idea to be away from home and to finally get some rest.

In our suitcases were clothes from the Goodwill Store, hats and gloves, plus long underwear, that I purchased at a great low price.

When we arrived at Homewood Ski Resort, we then rented skis, signed up for ski lessons, and rode the ski lifts into the heavens. I stayed down below in the safer, and friendlier area, until -- Bernadette skied down and told me how much fun the three were having, and how they wanted to share that fun with me.

The next thing I knew, I was being hauled against my will up and away on a ski lift, with no idea how I was ever going to get back down.

The experience was exhilarating. The views from the mountains were breathtaking. As I got higher, I could see all the green trees had turned pure white, a scene unbeknownst to me. "Heaven should be so beautiful". I could have never imagined such beauty. Had I not stepped out of my fear zone, I would have missed it all.

Going down the mountain on skis, with one lesson under my belt, was another story. Guided by my child, I maneuvered most of the time on my behind. I could have starred in one of the funniest home movies.

Learning from this experience, I realized I had other passions. I had a great passion for music and dancing. Therefore, I started to take piano lessons, and I joined a singles club where they offered free dance classes.

Chapter XXI
New Steps

"Fear of flying, get behind me."

My next step into the unknown that I took was in January 1980. I took a month's trip to *Campinas*, a city near *São Paolo*, Brazil, to spend some time with my wonderful friend, counselor, and brother, Lewie. I took a small loan, using my car as collateral, which at the time was out of character for me. As it turned out, my trip to Brazil will always be one of the best decisions of my life. That trip was a great healing time for me. Lewie loaded me up with books, but most of all, he showered me with unconditional love. We had always been this close.

I celebrated my 40th birthday in Brazil, February 1980, during a tour to *Iguaçu* Falls, which is located between Brazil, Argentina, and Paraguay. Lewie could not go with me on that weekend trip. He had a prior engagement to attend the graduation of a good friend. He encouraged me to go see the falls without him, by reminding me that I'd been a "big girl", by stepping out in courage, coming to Brazil on my own.

On my last week in Brazil, Lewie and I joined a tour group that included some of his friends to Rio de Janeiro, from where I'd be flying back to the U.S.

I said my good-byes to the two friends I had stayed with in Campinas, his best friend and former priest, Gil Avellar, and his wife, Celsa

We took an all-night bus trip from Campinas to Rio. As I sat on the bus, next to my sweet brother, the tears started to flow. I could not contain them as much as I tried. Hours later, Lewie broke the silence, turned to me, and said, "I know exactly how you feel. The first time I had to go home after living in Brazil for a few months, I also cried all the way from Rio to Miami. I was so touched by the Brazilian people and I knew how much I would miss them."

Lewie and I attended the Carnival in Rio, which is indescribable. Some of the groups in the many parades were members of dance schools that competed with one another, as they displayed their colorful costumes and their exotic dancing. The parades lasted all day and all night for the entire week.

We had the opportunity to visit some historic points, such as The *corcovado*, the tallest statue of Jesus in the world, Sugar Loaf Mountain, and *Ipanema* beach, the places Rio is so famous for.

As the tour in Rio ended, Lewie and two of his friends accompanied me to the airport for my trip home. They made sure I got on my flight before they headed back to Campinas.

They each had little trinkets for me--a small diary, and many postcards of the various places we'd visited.

When we said our good-byes, Lewie assured me he'd be back in the States in a few years, to spend some time with our elderly parents.

Lewie, an ordained Jesuit priest, had chosen to work with "the least of these," instead of as a parish priest.

Lewie learned about his ministry in Campinas, from his friend Gil. This ministry was started by the New Orleans Louisiana province Jesuits. They had started a business school called, *Centro Kennedy*, for men and women. This school empowered the less fortunate to become self-reliant. The motto of the school was, "Give a man a fish, he'll eat for a day. Teach him how to fish and he'll eat for a lifetime."

Lewie joined the business school in order to work with the homeless children from the streets of Campinas. He had great compassion for the young and the poor, and those rejected by society. He too, had come from poverty, which gave him even more compassion for those discarded by society through no fault of their own.

Lewie worked on the streets of Campinas, gathering the homeless children, visiting and comforting the sick, and giving hope to those that were hungry for self-acceptance and self-value.

It was during this time, that he was studying the Bible, and teaching others the culture at the time of Christ. His teachings included, the parables of the lost sheep, the lost coin, and the lost son. These are all examples of the Love of God, who seeks those who are in most need.

Lewie was loved by everyone he came in contact with. The youth felt valued. The adults, who at times had been suffering from guilt and shame, were blessed by the love of Jesus. Lewie taught and showed them this love, by telling them that God was not mad at them but that GOD was madly in love with them. I will never forget my time spent in Brazil.

*1980 Campos do Jordao, Brazil
Lewie and me*

Chapter XXII
Starting Over

When I returned to California, I continued with dance lessons. My instructor was a ballroom dancer. Watching him dance after class at the singles club with the best lady dancers was such a thrill. Fred Astaire would have bowed down to the great, suave, debonair dancer, Arthur Roy.

Much to my surprise, Art asked me to dance one night. Lucky for me, that first dance song was short because I felt like I had two left feet. We had both been divorced for a short time. We talked for a while after the dance. I told him about my trip, and we talked about golf, our new hobby. I continued my dance lessons with Art, and we always talked about golf. A couple of months later, we went out for coffee. Our first date was on Memorial Day weekend, 1980.

Art and I were married two years later on June 6, 1982. What captured me the most, and what I admired about this man from the start, was his honesty, sincerity, and zest for life.

Art was someone I could be honest and open with. He was an electronic engineer, and I was a full-charge bookkeeper. He continued to teach ballroom dancing at several colleges and lodges for many years, and I became his joint dance instructor. I also became a certified aerobics instructor, and taught aerobics for the YMCA in San Jose for several years. We joined several golf clubs and played all of the golf courses in Santa Clara County, and beyond.

I first heard about golf from some of my employers. I never imagined having the opportunities to be an avid golfer, play at so many golf courses, and in golf tournaments.

The same goes for ballroom dancing. I loved music and always wanted to learn to dance, which was forbidden in my youth. The opportunity to belong to ballroom dance clubs and dance in the most amazing ballrooms around the Bay Area, Southern California, Boston, and outside the U.S., was something beyond my dreams. Those luxuries, like many others, only existed in the movies, as far as I was concerned. They became my reality along with so many other blessings I've received in the beautiful part of the world called America.

Our Wedding 1982
Art and Me

Dad giving me away

Chapter XXIII
Explorations

Most of our travels were short trips that we took which always included golf. We also enjoyed trips to Hawaii and Mexico. For 20 years, we spent our vacations in Mazatlán and Cancun, Mexico, which we dearly loved. We went to mainland Portugal, where I had the opportunity, for the first time, to visit the monuments, palaces, and historical places I had learned about in the 4th grade. And yes, we even played golf in *Algarve*, the most beautiful coast in Portugal. Art and I went to the Azores together a few times. The first time I went back to my home town, was in 1996, 38 years after leaving that small village. My daughter, Lucinda, was my traveling companion. I finally had the chance to see the entire island for the first time. Instead of three cars in my village, that I was accustomed to, almost everyone had some type of transportation. The island even had tour guides for land and sea.

I remembered every field, every house, hill, and valley, when I came back to my village. This brought many fond memories back from my childhood. My daughter, some cousins, and I walked and hiked that island to our heart's content. Lucinda and I also visited the island Faial. In Faial, we met another cousin who was also visiting from California. Lucinda stayed in Faial with cousins while Tony and I decided to visit the island of Pico. We both had a dream to climb Pico Mountain, the highest volcanic mountain in Portugal, covered by nothing but rock and a few shrubs. This mountain is 7,700 feet in altitude, and a very dangerous one to climb. We tackled and conquered the expedition and sometimes crawling up the lava base of this amazing mountain. We found out later that the local authorities did not allow anyone to climb Pico without a guide. Ignorance is bliss. I'm so glad to have had the opportunity to view several of the Azores Islands from the top of Pico at one time, and to see the millions of stars that were as large as saucers, because we made it to the top at night fall.

I have always wanted to see more of America. To satisfy this wish, I've recently taken two trips across the country by auto and had the good fortune to visit 32 states of America.

My first visit to Washington D.C. was very memorable. Art and I had our two older grand kids with us, Cecily and Jarret, then 13 and 11. We first went to Philadelphia, Pennsylvania, and visited as many historic sites as we could. We then went to our nation's capital and visited the Smithsonian's museums and our National Monuments.

I also had the opportunity with a friend to visit Nashville, Tennessee, for the Red Hat Convention. While there, I went to a show at the Grand Ole Opry. I had fallen in love with country music since I arrived in America.

We attended a show at the Opry, but before I could go in the theater, I sat outside and had the best happy tears ever. I could not believe I was there -- an unimaginable dream come true for me.

Another trip Art and I took was a Mississippi River Cruise, which was an amazing historic voyage. We visited many of the old historic mansions/plantations, and learned so much about American history. We also visited the Civil War sites and monuments.

I went with a few girl friends on a four-day trip to Washington D.C. again and this time visited New York as well. A visit to Ellis Island and to the statue, Mother Liberty, was another emotional satisfaction for me.

All these journeys have been a great ride. I firmly believe that life is a trip, not a destination. I don't know when, or if I will ever arrive, but I sure have enjoyed each step of this wonderful voyage.

Washington D.C. 2003

Going to a dance

The Mayflower My immigration was not as difficult as this must have been for the pilgrims.

Golfing in Algarve Portugal with Russ and Mary Lee Blackburn. 1985

Mary Silveira and Me, A dream come true.

Chapter XXIV
The Family's Priest

"Who plucked that flower?" Asked the gardener.
"The Master," was the reply.
And the gardener held his peace."
John Bunyan

When Art and I got married, we both lived in the house on Bray Avenue. After a few months, we decided to sell our houses to buy a condo on Saratoga Avenue in Santa Clara. We lived in that condo for six years. In the summer of 1988, after all three of the children moved to start their own journeys, we sold the condo and purchased another home at The Villages Golf and Country Club in San Jose.

The weekend we were preparing to move to our dream home, November 11, 1988, we were also getting ready to attend a dinner dance in San Francisco. We received a phone call from the Saint Clare's parish in Santa Clara telling us there had been a shooting in Holland and that the pastor would be at my parents' house to give the family more details.

My brother Lewie had just left to the University of Utrecht to finish his doctorate degree in psychology, with a parapsychology background. Before he left, he was living at Santa Clara University for the last three years. He had been attending to our parent's needs of doctor's appointments, and grocery shopping. The University was down the road from my parents' house.

When we got to my parent's house, some of the other siblings were there, and the others arrived afterwards. I recall Dad's joy at seeing so many of his kids together. He kept saying, "Someone bring another chair."

After we were all there, none of us had suspected or could have guessed what we were about to hear. We were wondering about some political unrest, until the priest spoke.

Lewie had been killed by an assassin's bullet.

The first words from Dad's mouth were, "I never thought I would bury one of my children." Those words resonated deeply into our hearts. We all had children, and we understood the deep emotion our father felt.

My life, as well as the lives of our family members, stood still, for the next several weeks. This was the darkest time in my life. I would get up in the middle of the night and walk around the golf course next to the house. The course was far away from other homes, so no one heard me cry out to God. Many times Art would find me curled up into a ball, just wanting to die.

Ruth Bell Graham in her book "Legacy of a Pack Rat," Encouragement chapter, explains how most families, have an encourager. This encourager may not always be the oldest, younger, or middle child. He or she has innate sense of balance, and a good sense of humor. These two qualities almost invariably go hand in hand.

They are the encouragers. They keep in touch by note or phone call. They smooth things over when the going gets a little rough. They do not always share their own problems or hurts because they are too busy shouldering those of others.

Our family always turned to Lewie when we had issues and problems. He was steady, unassuming, and loyal, with remarkable wit and uncanny discernment. He was the family rallying point.

"Why, God? Why Lewie? People need more men like Lewie. He was greatly used by You to free so many of hurts, disappointments, guilt, and misunderstandings. You are supposed to be a good God. I don't see any good in his death"

After Lewie's body was flown home to Santa Clara, and as emotionally crippled as we all were, we decided to have a memorial of life, Lewie style. This style meant each of us took an active role in the Mass and readings as we had done when Lewie celebrated his first Mass ten years before, at Saint Clare's Church in Santa Clara.

Lewie had insisted that his first mass be a family celebration, and not the celebration of a new priest. He had everyone participate in each detail of the Mass and the preparation of this celebration. One family baked the bread to be broken for communion, another family made the wine. Part of his garments were made by the family women. All of Lewie's brothers and sisters, and our parents, were celebrants around the altar. Little did we know we'd be doing another memorial of life so soon.

One thing we did know, was that Lewie had asked for a dispensation from the priesthood, but while he waited for all the paperwork, he had been cut off from the Jesuit Order's financial support. He had taken on some part-time jobs and was counseling others to pay for his rent and his studies.

Lewie's friend in Holland, Maria José, told us that one of the young men he was counseling had visited Lewie one day and accused Lewie of brain washing him and threatened Lewie with his life. Lewie had shared that with Maria José and admitted to be frightened. She'd told my brother to "Ignore that kid. He's very mixed up."

Exactly one week later, on November 11, that young man made his threat come true, and changed our lives forever.

Letters and cards poured in from all over the United States and other countries where Lewie had worked, preaching the Gospel, the love of Jesus, and the hope we have in God.

Lewie had written a letter to his good friend, Father Bernardino Andrade, whom Lewie had worked with at the Portuguese cultural center in Hayward, California, and had asked him to share his letter with his parishioners. Father Bernardino responded with his blessings.

The pain and the loss all of us felt cannot be described. Over and above the deep pain, I felt angry, I was angry even at Lewie's colleagues and friends. "Why are they still alive, while our brother is dead."
Why God? Why him? He was only forty-one, our family needed him. The world needs more people like him.

Included in a condolence card sent to me by Doctor Augustine, was the book, "When Bad Things Happen to Good People," written by Harold Kushner. It answered so many questions I had been asking God.

My friend and editor, Sue Clark in her book "Tell Them I Loved Life," told us how her son Kyle asked her if she could answer the question they'd been seeking -- Why did our brother Brian have to die when his dreams were all coming true? He had a wonderful wife, his children were his pride and joy.

She told him, "I've finally found peace now that I realize God had other plans for your brother. I think Brian accomplished what God had planned for his life to be on earth, and it was time for him to leave. Brian brought joy to all those he came in contact with, and for whatever reason, they welcomed that joy and their lives are happier for it."

I realized that blaming God for the death of a loved one, is the reaction of most people. We need to blame something, or someone. However, doing so, also brings guilt, because deep down we know that God does not cause our tragedies.

The gospel tells us in Matthew 24:42, "Therefore be on the alert, for you do not know which day your Lord is coming." God's purpose is not our purpose. Jesus came to serve. He was a servant of God. My brother was Christ-like. His understanding and compassion of human beings was his best gift.

Lewie's remains were interred at Santa Clara Catholic Cemetery in the Jesuit's plot.

Lewie had done extensive studies on the culture of the Azores. Some of his papers and research can be found in the Santa Clara University Library, Archives Department.

Lewie was afraid to fly. I cannot count how many times we'd go to San Francisco Airport to say our good-byes. This tradition followed our family for many years. We'd take our parents, and there would always be a room full of "clowns" sending the bigger clown around the world. Even with his fear of flying, Lewie would not give up.

I tried to learn from Lewie, but it took a few years to muster the courage to get on a flying machine. It also took me several years and lots of counseling before I could have a dialogue with Lewie. Now, when I do fly, I talk to Lewie, and I tell him, "Go ahead and laugh all you want, you were afraid, too," as I tremble all the way to my destination.

First Mass 1979

The Last family photo with mom, dad, and all their children.

"Gifts from Spirit"
Doctor Augustine
Hearts fire Books 1997
pp, 236-239

On November 16, 1988 the San Jose Mercury-News carried a lead article that read "Priest Meets Death Helping Others." As I read on, I was shocked and dismayed to learn that the victim Lewie Dias, whom I had known briefly when he was a patient of mine. The article went on to say that Father Dias, age forty-one, had spent the past few years studying parapsychology for his doctorate at the University of Utrecht in Holland. He had been killed by a deranged student he had been counseling.

I had known Lewie and had felt him to be a warm and loving person. I addition to feeling sympathetic, I was curious as to how this tragedy could have come about. As I read on, I learned that Lewie had been planning to return to Brazil, where he had six years of his life helping to run a community clinic for medical and social services. The most touching recollection of Lewie was by his sister, Mary Roy (who had also been a patient of mine, who described a postcard Lewie had recently sent to his family. It showed a beautiful peacock and, on the other side, Lewie had written, "We must be like the peacocks and allow our inner beauty to come out, to enjoy and be grateful.")

After reading this, a deep part of me intensely shared in the family's grief, and lingered, as though a close and dear friend had died. Somehow, a part of me died when I learned of Lewis's death.

Maybe it had to do with the photos I had recently received, or maybe it was guilt. During the brief time I had treated Lewie he talked about the missionary work he had been doing in Brazil before continuing his postgraduate studies. Lewie told me he had been helping some native people, who were very poor and uneducated, in overcoming their fear of oppressive superstitions that he claimed was enslaving them and causing them grief. At that time, I was ambivalent, to say the least, about religion, and this caused me to oversimplify and over generalize. Mostly, I saw missionaries as merely providing the uneducated masses a new form of enslavement in exchange for their old one. Richard Bach, once said, "Whoever robs a man in order to rule him is not fit to be his ruler."

After reading about Father Dias, I realized that here was a man who had dedicated himself to helping others in the true Christian sense. He was no pampered, arm-chair priest, but a well-educated Jesuit who spoke seven languages and was always available for support and encouragement, in the most hopeless of circumstances and in the most distant of places-wherever he was needed. So the guilt I felt was the knowledge of how I had spent almost all my life making snap judgments and stereotyping people, regardless of who they really were. As a memorial to Father Dias, I vowed to try my best not to do that again, and I promised that I would visit his family, and give them my condolences, as soon as I could.

The photos I refer to were black and white photographs showing my father in a black priest's robe and collar. Dad had been initiated into the Catholic priesthood, briefly, during his young adulthood. When I had looked at these previously well-guarded photos, I realized that my father's young features were a spitting image of my own.

With the news of Father Dias death still fresh in my mind, I strongly felt that there was some connection in all of this.

Why had his death affected me so deeply? And why did I frame the photos of Dad in his Catholic vestments and display them on my desk, when I had spent most of my life running away from my birth faith?

Chapter XXV
Spiritual Gifts

"The Christian does not think God will love us because we are good, but that God will make us good because He loves us."
C. S. Lewis

In 1989, the famous Loma Prieta earthquake occurred and many financial changes took place in Northern California. Because of the massive damage to the apartment complex that we invested in and lack of enough reserves to repair the destruction from the earthquake, most of us investors lost "our shirts." Art and I were two of those investors at this time.

At that time, Art had retired from his engineering job, and the two rental houses we owned did not provide enough income to keep up with our mortgage payments, so we sold those properties. I still had my book keeping job, and Art and I still taught dancing two nights a week. However, the financial situation started to take a toll on our marriage.

Art was having regrets about retiring at the age of 59, and regrets of having made investment decisions without understanding the mechanics of the market.

I refused to cry over money. The loss of my brother had taught me a strong lesson about money, which is "there is no money that can compare to the value of life."

One Sunday morning, we attended a church service nearby our house, and we noticed they were offering a marriage conference for couples having relationship difficulties. We made an appointment and went to the conference, run by a priest in a large hotel in Mountain View. We listened to the testimonials of several couples, did the communication exercises given by the priest, and did the follow-up sessions on the next eight Saturdays, where a chosen topic was shared between each couple.

The very last Saturday, each couple was given a question to discuss between each other. "Where is God in your life?"

How could I answer that? Art and I had a beautiful home, we taught dance lessons and played golf at many clubs, made great friends, and had a healthy family. Who needs God?

Then, for reasons unknown, we received an invitation to visit a little "multi-denomination" church close by. We did, signed the visitor's card, and a few days later, we received a packet explaining the church's vision, and a tape of the pastor's testimonial. I put the tape in my car to listen on my way to work. I couldn't contain my tears, so much of the pastor's experiences in growing up paralleled mine.

Religion had taught me to obey priests, men, and rules to earn the Love of God, rather than receiving the Love of God first and wanting to obey Him because of His Love for me.

After receiving His Love into my heart, I know that nothing can separate me from that Love. Romans 8:37-39 *No, in all these things we are more than conquerors through him who loved us. For I am sure that neither death nor life, nor angels nor rulers, nor things present nor things to come, nor powers, nor height nor depth, nor anything else in all creation, will be able to separate us from the love of God in Christ Jesus our Lord.*

What this means to me is that God loves us unconditionally no matter what. I have been asked why I abandoned my religion, as if abandoning religion is the same as rejecting God.

Quoting from "Gifts from Spirit," Doctor Augustine wrote.

All life is a spiritual journey, and all growth is spiritual growth whether the individual realizes it or not. But rarely family members or close friends or acquaintances are on the same part of the spiritual journey at the same time. This may explain at least some of the lack of harmony in the world. And unless the persons involved have all traveled far enough along the path so that there is an appreciation and respect for the process, spiritual growth can and often does cast relationships asunder.

Thus the irony. As those on the spiritual path grow in their ability to love, beloved ones who are on an earlier stretch of the path may be unable to receive it and may even turn from it in confusion, alarm or hostility.

Since that marriage conference, Art and I have dedicated ourselves to learning more about the Christian faith by studying the Word of God. We have found an immense peace that passes all understanding. Above all, that peace has released me from the guilt that was at the center of my upbringing -- condemnation, fear, and shame. I'm only learning to realize that the God of the Universe loves us all, equally and unconditionally.

The amazing thing about hurts, rejection, even tragedies are, they bring us to a closer relationship with God and help us with our spiritual growth.

> *"Within the covers of the Bible are the answers for all the problems men face."*
> *Ronald Reagan*

Chapter XXVI
The American Dream

So many times my dad would talk about the "American dream," which he really believed he had achieved, not for himself, but for his children and their children's children.

He'd say over and over how grateful he was that he brought his family out of poverty to a land filled with opportunity. My father moved from a world that did not encourage personal achievement to a world that puts no limits on achievement. He was told that a man was only worth the daily ration of bread that he eats per day. He was fortunate to live long enough to see all his children married and to meet his 32 grandchildren and 20 great grandchildren. He passed away at the age of 92. Mom preceded him by five years.

Several of Dad's grandchildren are college graduates. They range in education from school teachers, engineers, and auto mechanics, a medical student, and even a United States Postmaster. And if I may say, Godly men and women.

Two of Dad's grand kids, Elizabeth and Frankie, wrote the following eulogy, which Frankie read at their grandfather's memorial.

Manuel Batista Dias was stern, honest, and strong of character. When it came time for us grand kids to get married, he made sure to remind the newlywed-to-be that he and Avo' attended a novena at church on their wedding night. C'mon, Avô, you had eleven kids! Of course, you didn't hear anyone say that to his face!

He raised his children, and about half of his grandchildren, to be God-fearing, law-abiding citizens. He'd even make his own laws as the years went by. You weren't allowed to use his sidewalk, park in front of his house, or watch TV in his presence. He had creative ways of making you pay the consequences:

If you were his neighbor and parked next to his house, letting the oil from the car drip on HIS Street, He'd paint the curb red and let you try and explain it to the police why you're in a no parking zone!

But the TV...Oh, the TV...He hated it so much he actually insisted on keeping it covered with a blanket. When his roommate at the rest home had the audacity to watch it, Avô got up and broke the TV with his cane!

This man could scare the devil himself! He was something else and will be sorely missed. There is so much more to say; so many other stories to share. Just ask any of his nine remaining children, 32 grand-children, or 29 great-grandchildren.

We'll always remember his cane and the way he'd hook your neck as you tried to sneak by him, the sound of his laughter, though creaky from lack of use, and just his presence. As intimidated by him as we all were, you were just drawn to him. He demanded our respect.

We'll always remember you, Avô Palhaça.

1982 Manuel and Clara Dias 50th Wedding Anniversary.

Chapter XXVII
The American Hero

Three generations in our family gave us military heroes, who served our country in the Marine Corps and in the Army with honor and pride. Two of these heroes are my brothers Frank and Manuel who served in the Vietnam War.

The Elias Brothers

William
U S ARMY

Leonel
U S ARMY

This nation will remain the land of the free only so long as it is the home of the brave.

Ralph
U S ARMY

The Dias Brothers

Manuel Dias
U S MARINE

Frank Dias
U S MARINE

My son

If our country is worth dying for in time of war let us resolve that it is truly worth living for in time of peace

John Paul Cabral
U S MARINE

My Nephews and Niece

Jaime Avila
U S MARINE

Frank Dias Jr
U S MARINE

Britany and Justine Dias
U S ARMY

Chapter XXVIII
America The Beautiful

Poverty in America vs the rich of my native land, Azores, was often a topic that Dad and I loved to talk about. I want to share some of the comparisons we made together in our conversations.

Those few that we called rich in the Azores, may have had their servants, but they had nothing compared to what the poor people of America have right here and now. Here, there are many more luxuries and comforts such as running water and electricity. These Americans who think they are poor have air conditioned houses, with screens to keep the bugs out. They have milk all year round, and they never have to feed the cow or make sure it is healthy. How about eggs? There is no need to collect them or clean them. In the Azores we would have to take them to the market to trade for other commodities like detergent to wash our clothes. In America, we just eat them. How about a stove? In America we press a button, put a pot on the stove and start cooking. Growing up we had to carry the wood from miles away to burn under the pot. Bread? What type? In the US there's wheat, corn, sour dough, even sweet bread, available on any day of the week. There is fruit, marvelous fruit, all year long in our nation. Another gift is Music. Here we have beautiful music, available everywhere, on radio, television, or iPod. Telephone? There is no need to wait a month or more to hear from your loved ones.

How about washing and drying clothes? In America we do not need to travel to the nearest river to beat our clothes against rocks and to dry them in the sun. The luxuries the American poor have also include medical and dental care. My family never visited a dentist or a doctor while growing up. All Americans, rich or poor, are blessed by living in the greatest country called the United States of America.

We are all victors and not victims, and we are endowed by our Creator by so much more that we can think of or ask of Him. Above all, our freedoms, that come only from God our Father, is our greatest gift. For this freedom, He alone deserves the Glory.

When I came to America, I started to study its short history. To realize how great a country America is, does not take a college degree in

History. Our Founding Fathers designed our country where people can be free to pursue their happiness: "Life, Liberty and the pursuit of Happiness"

These are the greatest gifts given to man that only come from the Creator's Hand. What God has given; the State should not take away.

To be truly free, we must believe that our freedoms come from God Himself, not from men or governments. If we do not believe that this is the foundation of our freedom, then we are on sinking sand and any one can take our freedoms away. "We hold these truths to be self-evident, that all men are created equal, that they are endowed by their Creator with certain unalienable Rights, that among these are Life, Liberty and the pursuit of Happiness".

The Bible had a lot influence on the Founding Fathers of America. That is because it is the Words of God Almighty Himself. Most of them believed this truth. We are still Under Him as one Nation!

America the Beautiful, as I like to call her, is one of the greatest gifts to humanity. She is the mother who embraces you, regardless of your background, adopts you, and calls you daughter or son. She also encourages you to thrive, to learn, to grow, and to be all that God created you to be. America is also a teacher. All though she instructs, she also learns from you. Side-by-side, hand-in-hand, we the people can grow together in knowledge and beauty.

This realization is what makes me so grateful for being in America. I left my Mom, Dad, 10 siblings, a huge family, and many friends at the age of 19. I cringe now, as I fathom a high school-aged teen, leaving behind all she knew, with only a hope and a prayer.

Regardless of anyone's financial status, rich, poor or in between, our value as human beings go above and beyond what money can buy. What is our worth? The Word of God says over and over that we were bought and paid for with the most expensive price ever paid. We are not worth what we happen to think, or any "low-ball" offer. We are worth what the highest bidder will pay and has paid. The highest bidder is God, and the price-tag is the Cross the Death of His Son. God looked out across the eternal ages and said, "I'll take that one, even though the price is steep!" Our worth is established once and for all, and can never change or diminish. God has made the ultimate offer and paid the highest price for you. We were saved with the precious blood of Jesus, the Son who gave us so many examples of the value of our life. To Love Him is now easy and freeing in this life.

Ronald Reagan said, "America has been the most successful country in world history. I believe that our success and the blessings given to this country, is from God. He is the source of our nation's prosperity, and to forget this truth, is to bring demise to our land". Moses told his people this truth that still applies to us today. Deuteronomy 8:7-11, *7 For the LORD your God is bringing you into a good land—a land with brooks, streams, and deep springs gushing out into the valleys and hills; 8 a land with wheat and barley, vines and fig trees, pomegranates, olive oil and honey; 9 a land where bread will not be scarce and you will lack nothing; a land where the rocks are iron and you can dig copper out of the hills. 10 When you have eaten and are satisfied, praise the LORD your God for the good land he has given you. 11 Be careful that you do not forget the LORD your God, failing to observe his commands, his laws and his decrees that I am giving you this day. ,*

I thank God for all of His gifts, and I pray I never forget the One who gives the gifts because it is too easy to keep my eye on the gifts and not the Giver. President Abraham Lincoln, during the Civil War, called for a national day of repentance and prayer. He warned Americans of the sin of pride. He said, "We have been the recipients of the choicest bounties of Heaven. We have been preserved, these many years, in peace and prosperity. We have grown in numbers, wealth and power, as no other nation has ever grown. But we have forgotten God. We have forgotten the gracious hand which preserved us in peace, and multiplied and enriched and strengthened us; and we have vainly imagined, in the deceitfulness of our hearts, that all these blessings were produced by some superior wisdom and virtue of our own. Intoxicated with unbroken success, we have become too self-sufficient to feel the necessity of redeeming and preserving grace, too proud to pray to the God that made us." Looking at my nation today, I see history repeating itself. United we stand, Divided we will fall as a nation. Can we change this course we are on?

My friend, Dr. Ben Gilmore, made the following observation. "Many today have lost sight of, or never discovered, the exceptionality of this Nation. God's hand in human history is a 6000 year story of His teaching men how to love Him and how to get along with one another. That story climaxed with the creation of the first nation in human history to establish itself upon Godly principles. If this experiment in Christian self-government fails, it will appear that God's principles do not work. The world will be swept with hopelessness. America, I believe, will survive. Not indeed for our sake, but for God's sake, and for what it means to the world He loves. I can envision God sitting on the edge of His throne, anxiously watching to see if there are enough of us in prayer and action to justify His mercy over justice"

I thank God for all the opportunities I have encountered in this country, and I thank God for our ancestors who sacrificed so much so that we could enjoy better lives than they had. May we never forget them, and may we always remember to live in gratefulness.

"My dream is of a place and a time where America will once again be seen as the last best hope of earth."
Abraham Lincoln

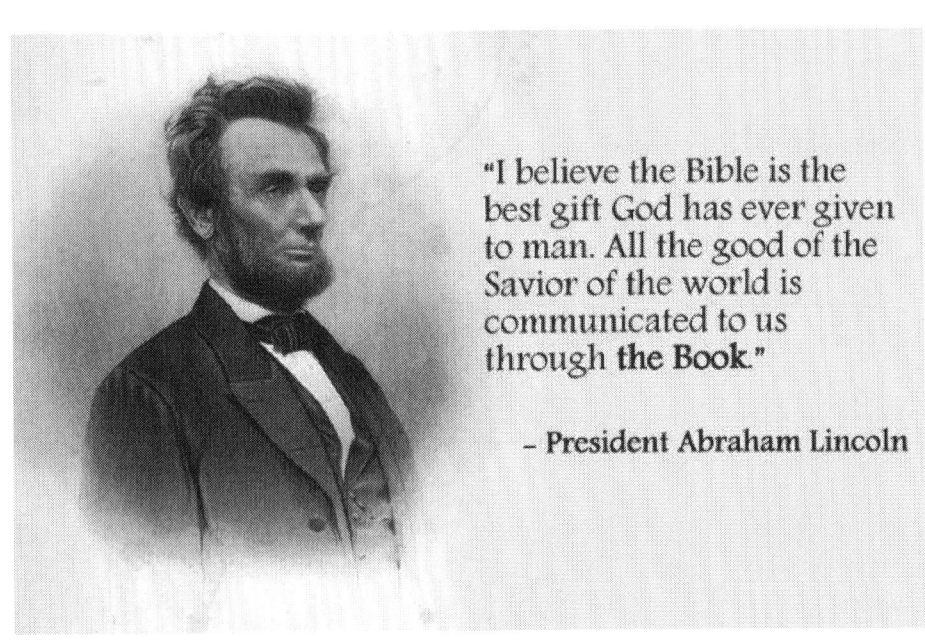

"I believe the Bible is the best gift God has ever given to man. All the good of the Savior of the world is communicated to us through the Book."

— **President Abraham Lincoln**

Coming to America

This is the first song I learned and played at my first piano recital in 2010. Thank You to my piano instructor Coralee for teaching me and for all those hours of support and friendship.

Appendix A
Friendships

I cannot go on with my memoir without mentioning the most valuable gift of my entire life, the gift of friendship, without which there could be no meaning or point in living. I was fortunate to experience friendship at a young age with a lady named Connie, which gave me the courage I would need, to navigate the road of life.

Connie's husband, Sam, was one of the engineers at Gangi Bros. in Santa Clara, where I worked. He supervised the making of the product, -- tomato paste, tomato ketchup, pizza sauce, -- and I was at the end of the line, doing the quality control in the lab. We communicated by phone between lab and production.

Sam had heart disease. During Sam's heart surgery is when I first met Connie. When we met, we instantly hit it off and knew that our friendship was not going to be a casual friendship. We prayed together and cried many tears during Sam's surgery. It still amazes me when I think about my friend and how much she taught me about the meaning of real friendship. She showed me that Love is the foundation of true friendship.

Even though I was married, had three small children, I had not attained that level until I met her. The more I shared myself with Connie, the more I felt accepted by her. I enjoyed the depth of our friendship and realized how important we were to each other. I became a better person because of who she was, and how we interacted with each other. I always thought of her as a mom, maybe due to our age difference. She was like a mom, and she loved me as a daughter. I learned that to love another person, means to accept him or her regardless of faults. I certainly was not a perfect human being and felt undeserving of her love. I also learned that two people can have different views and beliefs, and still have a deep friendship.

There were times we both dialed each other at the same moment. One Friday evening, about 6:00 p.m., we had a short conversation that ended with "I love you." That was our last conversation. September of 1978, my world came crumbling down. Connie had a major heart attack that stole my reason for living. I honestly believed I could not live without her. I soon realized her loving memory would be with me and encourage me.

Connie knew me very well inside and out. When she learned about my desire to get a real estate license, she offered to lend me the money needed for Real Estate School. I attended the Anthony School of Real Estate. I took a vacation day per week in order to attend the lectures and take the practice tests. I also passed the Real Estate Board test on the first try. I then started working for Tony Matos at Red Carpet Realty in Santa Clara that lasted for over four years.

I have a greeting card Connie once sent me. Inside is the following poem.

"I looked for my soul, but my soul I could not see.
I looked for my God, but my God eluded me.
I looked for a friend, and then I found all three."

John Powell, in "The Secret of Staying in Love" wrote,
"It is an absolute human certainty that no one can know his own beauty or perceive a sense of his worth until it has been reflected back to him in the mirror of another loving, caring human being."

Thank You Connie, for the gift of friendship, you will always be in my heart.

I looked for my soul
but my soul I could not see.

I looked for my God
but my God eluded me.

I looked for a friend
and then I found
all three.

~ William Blake

Appendix B

A Prayer for the Nation
Washington D.C.

Almighty God, Who has given us this good land for our heritage; We humbly beseech You that we may always prove ourselves a people mindful of Your favor and glad to do Your will. Bless our land with honorable ministry, sound learning, and pure manners. Save us from violence, discord, and confusion, from pride and arrogance, and from every evil way. Defend our liberties, and fashion into one united people, the multitude brought forth out of many generations and languages. Endow with Your Spirit of wisdom those who in Your name we entrust the authority of government, that there may be justice and peace at home, and that through obedience to Your law, we may show forth Your praise among the nations of the earth. In time of prosperity fill our hearts with thankfulness, and in the day of trouble, suffer not our trust in You to fail; all of which we ask through Jesus Christ our Lord. Amen.

Appendix C
Letters

Letter from Lewis Dias to Father Bernardino Andrade, plus Father Andrade's reply.

Holland, February 11, 1988

My dearest friend Bernardino:
As a father and a mother are responsible for their children, a Priest is also expected to satisfy his responsibility.
I feel very connected with the people that frequent the Portuguese Pastoral Center in Hayward. It was there that I have shared so much kindness and a tremendous out pour of love from so many people. It is now my turn to share with that community, a tremendous difficult and important phase of my life, and I will try to do it with the least amount of words as possible.
I would like to ask you to publish this in your bulletin, "Viver Como Irmãos," Living as Brothers. I hope and pray it would be "heard with the ears, but listened with the heart."
My dear friends of the Pastoral Center, especially all of you who participated in several course, given by me: "Bible, Feminism and the Holy Spirit, Psychology and Health, Parapsychology, Culture and Faith" etc.
I wish to announce that I will continue to work with Gods People, but in a different way. Not as a Priest.
Since childhood and above all the Vietnam War as well as other important motives, I made a decision somewhat voided of total personal freedom. Finally, after much prayer and after consulting several of those who have helped me so much and for so long, I decided to leave the Priesthood.
It has been a painful decision, but I know that God expects us to be honest. I have not felt totally convinced of my vocation, even though I have done everything in my power in order to be a faithful servant.
I worked more than ten years with the poor in Brazil, five years with the inmates, (three in San Quentin and two in Spokane, Washington,) and another three years with Latin American Immigrants in San Francisco.

When we make this type of decision, we lose. Sometimes, many friends, and even the financial help from those we love very much and who loved us also. Certainly, when this happens it simply means, people take things too serious and do not understand the significance of change.

When the Vatican threatened to abolish the Jesuit order, Saint Ignatius of Loyola, the founder of the Jesuit priest, said: "If the Jesuit order gets abolished by the mother church, it will only be necessary 15 minutes of prayer, for me to accept that decision with peace and a new vision in mind." The Jesuits were oppressed for a period of 80 years. During that time, they received help from Russia, until a more open minded Pope allowed the order to be reestablished.

Well, I am in peace with my decision, but I also feel much sadness for having lost many friends. But…What can I do? I have to respect their feelings too. They loved me as a Priest, not as Lewis. So sorry. Above all, I feel happy and extremely grateful for the support and kindness of so many.

My parents wrote and told me: "Son, you chose that life, we never forced you. The important thing is that Jesus continues to be your friend." I found these words to be so marvelous from parents that are at the ages of 77 and 79 years of age. Even though they are devout Catholics and faithful to the Church, they accepted my decision.

Until the second century of Christianity, the priest was elected only for a period of time, until the people elected a new priest. The outgoing priest would exercise other functions of ministry. It was then never the intention of the priest to stay in the same function. After the Vatican II the church has given dispensation to many priests, thus giving them the authority to choose a new life style.

I continue with my studies. I have a doctorate degree in Psychology, and now I am doing a doctorate in Psychology with Parapsychology background. My intention is to return to Brazil and work with the people there.

I work a little here. I have a few counseling clients, and I wash dishes in a restaurant, a few hours per week. I love working regardless what I do. I feel like an Immigrant. I am healthy, I study, I have faith and good attitude.

Friends, I thank you from the bottom of my heart, all of you who have helped me and supported me. I hope to continue being brothers in Christ. I expect one day soon to return to Hayward and offer various courses from what I have been learning.

I keep receiving the bulletin *"Viver Como Irmãos,"* It's marvelous.

Bernardino, accept my simple words, they are from the heart. I love you very much, may God bless you always.
Lewis Dias

Reply from Father Bernardino to Lewie
Hayward, February 23, 1988
Dearest Lewis:
    Thank you for sharing with us this difficult and important phase of your life. It is a privilege for me, and I am sure for many friends here to have the opportunity to be with you on this painful path. Our lives are just that. A cross on one side, and the Easter candle on the other. Don't be afraid. We loved Father Lewis Dias very much, but above all, we loved Lewis Dias, and …we believe that those who stopped being your friend, it's because they never were. You will not lose any friend.
    You captivated the hearts of this community, with all you knew and shared. What we learned from you about Parapsychology and about faith, was so new that I'm convinced that it touched us deeply in the way of thinking and living with one another, those who were fortunate enough to attend those courses, will never forget that gift. The comfortable way you'd open the Bible and talked about God, touched the hearts of all of us. Your knowledge, the simplicity, the sense of humor, and your faith in a "God the Father and God the Mother," your preference for the poor, our option for a Communitarian and liberating church. All of that and much more, created deep friendships in a people that not only loved you but will always continue to love and speak of you with kindness. It was so loving to hear you speak of a new church without attacking any one. In your heart everyone had a place: The ones who wanted a renewed church, a liberating church through the base communities, and those that wanted a structured, traditional church. Our faith grew so much when you'd refer to Mother-God. My references were always Father-God. It was with you that I learned to see Him as a Mother, and learned of your tenderness and affection and compassions that only mothers understand and know how to give. God is all that and much more.
    Come and visit us and you will see for yourself.
    When I received your letter, I called your parents. I spoke to Clara, that lady who always treated me like her son. We have a date on Wednesday,

Father Jose Maria and I will have lunch with your parents, and of course talk about you. I am anxious to hug those beautiful elderly, precious folks.

Goodbye Lewis. May God the Mother bless you. Hugs with much affection.

Bernardino

Appendix D
The Last Letter

Lewie's letter to me dated November 9, 1988
I had written him a letter on the same date reassuring him that my love for him would always go beyond the title after his name, whether he'd decide to stay a priest or not, I loved the person in him and I made the decision to support him in whatever he'd choose to do with his life. After all, Lewie had told me once, "Your life was given to you only, and it's up to you to use it to the best of your abilities."

Dear Sis and Art:

This is not a letter -- just a "visit." I have been invited by the Jesuits to visit the family in the summer or this Christmas and to settle the financial side with the Jesuits. I might have to wait until the summer. I am full-time in classes and I have 5-6 counselling clients per week. I am earning little, but it's mine. I feel proud. I do it all in Dutch.
It was scary, but we Dias' learn to love it in the end. So, I will spend time with all of you next summer. The Big Jesuit Superior from Rome went to California to tell them to treat me Royally. So, they can't do anything to hurt me anymore. I rented one of my rooms to a fellow student, so, now I can eat better and pay the rent and utilities, etc.
After California I'll go to Brazil for three months to do field work and see all my friends. Mary and Art, I pray for you and your kids. I trust all will go really well with all of them.
Love, Lewie
PS Bush won!! He'll do okay.

Children are God's gifts to us, and God's way of telling us that life goes on after we're gone.

Grandchildren are second chances at appreciating those gifts.

Grandchildren have their own parents to be concerned with them, most grandparents' functions is to love them, spoil them and enjoy them.

Both children and grandchildren are life's miracles.

    I am blessed beyond words for those miracles. I have received a tremendous amount of love from each and every one of them, and I love them unconditionally. I hope and pray that they know and believe that there is nothing they can ever do that will change the love I have for them. Above all, I hope they know that God is their Heavenly Father and loves them even more.

    I would give my life for any one of my children and grandchildren.

    God already did that for all of them.

Appendix E
My Most Precious Gifts

My Children: Lucinda, John, and Bernadette

Grandkids:

Rachel
Jarret
Cecily
Dominic
Jessica

Mary Roy's Coming to America

As a "TCK" (Third Culture Kid) who spent my years from birth to eighteen in the middle of Africa. I especially appreciated Mary Roy's perspectives on her own childhood - a rich heritage of family, traditions, culture, and language – and the abrupt change of scenery for her at the age of eighteen.

Eighteen-year-olds entering a new country – with the prospect of remaining there the rest of their lives – are simply expected to be happy, well-adjusted people. Others rarely discern the inner psycho-social struggle that we are experiencing. Mary's accounts of her life as an immigrant give us new appreciation of the clashes of consciousness that often remain hidden behind our attempts to appear to be just "normal" people.

Dr. H. Douglas Brown
Emeritus Professor of English
San Francisco State University

About the Author
Mary Roy

Mary Roy, a retired accountant, Realtor and mother, came to America in 1959, as an eighteen year old with only four years of grammar school education. Achieving the American Dream meant to make ends meet by working as a housekeeper, cannery worker, field worker by picking fruit, doing janitorial work. She also took in sewing and ironing.

In America, Mary found the opportunities and the freedom she'd sought to make her childhood dreams come true.

Mary and her husband live in Lincoln, California.

Final Words
Live your Dream

I'm an Immigrant from S. Jorge, Azores. I came to America in 1959, I was 19 years old, married and had 4 years of grammar school education.

I raised 3 children who were involved in LUSO and in the Portuguese philharmonic band---thanks to the efforts of other immigrants who created those opportunities for them.

I am also a grandmother of five grandchildren.
Several years ago I felt the need to share with all the children, my childhood memories from a life so different from theirs. I started to write down some notes, which led me to a writing class and ultimately I gathered those notes and stories, and here they are….. in my book "COMING TO AMERICA, AN IMMIGRANT'S VOYAGE".

My love for literature was limited to read, read and then read some more. The love of reading was instilled in me at an early age by my mom and grandmother. They read me stories from books borrowed from our parish priest, because of a lack of libraries, magazines etc....

I love books. Books have been my best friends. They have been my source of faith, courage, and inspiration.

I hope my book inspires others to write their stories. If I can do it with my limited education, anybody can do it. If we wait until we acquire all the knowledge and education until we do something, we'll never do anything. Iyanla Vazant, is an inspirational speaker and she wrote:

"It is important that we share our experiences with other people. Your story will heal you and your story will heal someone else. When you tell your story, you free yourself and give others permission to acknowledge their own story."

Whatever your goal and desire is, keep doing what you love.
Write a book—become a school teacher—become a doctor—Climb Mount Everest. Keep that dream alive, only you can reach that mountain top. "Every mountain top is within reach---If you just keep climbing". Gaze at the high point---It is yours to conquer.

Writing a book takes time and dedication. It also takes an immense amount of support and encouragement, without which it would be impossible to achieve. I want to thank all those who supported me throughout my journey. To all those that have walked with me side by side encouraging me all the way through,

"Thank You!"

Made in the USA
San Bernardino, CA
06 April 2016